T0004898

THE DEVIL'S NOTEBOOK
ANTON SZANDOR LAVEY

FERAL HOUSE

The Devil's Notebook © 1992 by Anton Szandor LaVey

All Rights Reserved:

ISBN 978-0-922915-11-8

21   27

Feral House
1240 W. Sims Way #124
Port Townsend, WA 98368

www.feralhouse.com
info@feralhouse.com

NOTE: Feral House is not the Church of Satan.

Church of Satan contact information:

Church of Satan
P.O. Box 499
Radio City Station, NY 10101
www.churchofsatan.com

Acknowledgements: Special thanks to Blanche Barton and Adam Parfrey
for the assistance and insistence that brought these writings aboveground.
— Anton Szandor LaVey

Dedicated to the men, whoever they are, who invented the
Whoopee Cushion, the Joy Buzzer, and the Sneeze-O-Bubble,
and to
John Taliaferro Thompson.

By Anton Szandor LaVey

The Satanic Bible
The Satanic Rituals
The Satanic Witch
The Devil's Notebook

About Anton Szandor LaVey

The Secret Life of a Satanist
The Authorized Biography of Anton LaVey
(by Blanche Barton)

The Church of Satan
(by Blanche Barton)

The Devil's Avenger
(by Burton Wolfe)

Speak of the Devil
(a video documentary by Nick Bougas)

Contents

Introduction

ALTHOUGH HIS BOOKS HAVE SOLD OVER A MILLION COPIES, THE PUBLISHING industry has chosen to ignore Anton LaVey. The book trade publication, *Publishers Weekly,* has never reviewed a publication by or about Anton LaVey. Aside from the occasional hysteria-inciting pieces that attempt to "expose" or "debunk" the founder of the Church of Satan, the print and electronic media have chosen to enforce a blackout on the true nature of his writings. Most of the so-called "alternative" press has taken the lead of the mainstream press not to confront the work or life of Anton LaVey, to wish him into non-existence. Why?

In a word, fear. The mainstream fears Christian opprobrium and ridicule. The politically correct individual fears the rapacity of his own id. Occultniks are threatened by LaVey's refusal to indulge their penchant for obscurantist mumbo-jumbo.

In our increasingly regimented egalitarian society, someone of Anton LaVey's flamboyance must be shunned, cut down to size. Unlike today's blue-jeaned, homiletic politicians, Anton LaVey does not allow Joe Citizen to feel comfortable in his workaday drabness. To the contrary. Whenever Joe Citizen confronts the spectre of this contemporary Ming the Merciless, he is reminded of forbidden pleasures that he was too cowardly to grab, of a life he was too circumspect to live. In his rationalizations, Joe Citizen pins a Goodguy Badge on his lapel and projects righteous derision on the object of his discomfort. "That Anton LaVey, what a phony!"

Perhaps it is time the Devil is given his due — thanks to LaVey the public has rediscovered "incredibly strange" films and music, such as *Freaks, Nightmare Alley,* the theremin and evocative tunes from the 1930s and 1940s, LaVey contributed several of the more celebrated photos in Kenneth Anger's *Hollywood Babylon,* LaVey coined the term "psychic vampire," among others, LaVey's automata have inspired research and development in the fields of robotics and teledildonics. Perhaps most importantly, no other man has so well illuminated the shadow purpose of Western life in the latter half of the twentieth century.

As LaVey has stressed over and over again, Satanism is not about heavy metal music or the sacrifice of children or animals to a horned deity. These are antics for the weak and confused. Anton LaVey's brand of Satanism involves a far more difficult and bracing task — the *realpolitik* application of principles that favors accomplishment over consumerism and individual power over herd mentality. LaVey's Satanism eschews all pandering to fads. It is less a movement than a call to recognition. I have one suggestion. Read LaVey for what he *says,* and not for what others say he *is.* May the scales fall from your eyes.

Adam Parfrey
October 1992

Foreword

IT'S AMAZING HOW MUCH FEAR IS INVOKED IN OTHERS BY THE PRESENCE OF A known Satanist. People who never advertise their religious backgrounds, when confronted by a "Devil worshipper" suddenly become devout. How often I see crosses around the necks of those who've been informed of my arrival — as if, like Lugosi's Dracula, I will be rendered powerless. And when I'm not fazed by such precautions, the aroma of nervous sweat really fills the room. It's then that I feel sadistic, if that term ever applied. I love to see those dusty crucifixes salvaged from the bottoms of bureau drawers, unworn since catechism. The evangelical bumper stickers that might just as well say "kick me." The little gold crosses. The pathetic victims of Christian propaganda wearing the symbol of their role model's death around their necks like tiny electric chairs or gas chambers or hangman's nooses, actually believing it will protect them. Protect them from what? My possible cordiality and friendship?

Wearing a display of dormant faith allows them to be safe — as safe and sure as their advertised deodorant — to ask me about Satanism. What is it like to be frightened of intangibles? I've never known, because I've always had my share of very real threats to my serenity. I took up Satanism not out of desperation but logical dismay that there were so many short-sighted people around me. I thought, acted, and thereupon found myself removed. And lo and behold, I was a Satanist. A prideful outcast. If the "just," the "good," the "righteous" were exemplified by the cowering ones, I wanted no part of them.

My brand of Satanism is the ultimate conscious alternative to herd mentality and institutionalized thought. It is a studied and contrived set of principles and exercises designed to liberate individuals from a contagion of mindlessness that destroys innovation. I have termed my thought "Satanism" because it is most stimulating under that name. Self-discipline and motivation are effected more easily under stimulating conditions. Satanism means "the opposition" and epitomizes all symbols of nonconformity. Satanism calls forth the strong ability to turn a liability into an advantage, to turn alienation into exclusivity. In other words, the reason it's called Satanism is because it's fun, it's accurate, and it's productive.

The following collection of essays, bits and pieces representing 25 years of diabolical thought, is a Satanic literary exercise in the strictest sense. Each segment is an indulgence of a whim or fancy. Each was written as the mood or idea manifested itself, whether spontaneously or gradually. No concern was given to whether or not what was written would be good, bad, offensive, pleasing, or even whether it would see print. Each was set to paper because to refrain from doing so would have meant self-denial.

Essays that are bitter were composed with a need to ritualized bitterness, the setting, form and style landing as the cards were dealt. Instructional or theoretical essays emerged, first as ideas which had to be recorded, then as written essays. Some have been gathering dust for many years and are included because timing demands that they be released. If they have been updated slightly, it is because popular folly has necessitated that comparisons be drawn. A Devil's Notebook must contain divergent observations and paradoxical theories. Like life itself, it is consistent in its inconsistency.

Anton Szandor LaVey
Durango, Mexico
31 August XXVII Anno Satanas

THE DEVIL'S NOTEBOOK

Hell must be a pretty swell spot, because the
guys that invented religion have sure been
trying hard to keep everybody else out.
— Al Capone

A Medicine for Melancholy
or
How to Avoid the DP'S

AT NO TIME IN WESTERN CIVILIZATION HAS MAN ACCEPTED SO WILLINGLY contrivances calculated to weaken and destroy him.

Many persons have found these years, as we approach the superstitious dread of the coming millennium, to be the most tumultuous period of their lives. Upheaval, depression, disillusionment, paranoia, anguish, anxiety, illness, and every other sort of malaise imaginable. Yeats' poem, "The Second Coming," expresses the social climate well. Surely an explanation, or at least speculation, is in order.

Let's examine some ingredients. No overseas war is in progress which involves Americans on a personal level, patriotic or otherwise. There is no universal enemy to occupy the minds and emotions of society. Hence enemies, threats, and other problems must emerge from a diversity of sources which are timely and easily relatable. Media re-enforcement of fears and anxieties is at an all-time zenith. Prime-time TV dispenses suspense and crisis, either real (newscasts) or by fictional or documentary features and series. This is considered "entertainment," not demoralization.

If complaints are voiced that streets are unsafe to stroll, surfs unsafe for swimming, and even grazing laid unsafe for cows ("Satanic Cattle Mutilation"), where can one expose his or her puny human form? In the safety of an automobile? Perhaps, but what of the subliminal demoralization coupled with a sense of false security that mandatory safety devices provide?

Despite rapid and radical advances in medicine, why are more people sick? Emphasis on prompt detection of certain symptoms is supposed to prevent serious illness. With everyone listening for internal gurgles, feeling for lumps, and pondering each pain, hypersensitivity cannot be avoided. Does a consuming concern for diet and exercise make for healthier living than sitting in the car gobbling Big Macs? Which takes a greater toll — fear of the effects of preservatives, chemical-pumped chicken, mercury-saturated fish — or the foods themselves?

If you are a law-abiding citizen, who is concerned about the safety of your home and family, you are made to feel like a criminal if you own a gun and are henceforth categorized as a "crazed gunman with a Saturday Night Special." Though you know you are responsible and conscientious, you are demoralized into stigmatization, nonetheless.

In bygone days, before you were demoralized by static cling, it was halitosis or B.O. or unsightly snaps or non-Sanforized Gaposis. How easy it would be if one needed only to fret over such trivial social ostracisms. Now, in addition to ring-around-the-collar, you are confronted by threats to your immune system, germ warfare, telephone bugging, new cancer viruses, conspiratorial politicians acting as decoys for the Real Rulers, governmental breakdown, danger in the streets, on the freeways, at the beach, rising costs of food, gasoline, higher taxes, and ... the unknown! Is another world watching? Are UFO's about to land in your front yard? And to The Good the threat of Satanism is still fine scare copy.

How to immunize yourself against the great D.P. (Demoralization Process) which is inexorably reaching its plateau?

1) Recognize it for what it is: a collective phenomenon, self-perpetrating according to Malthusian law. The separation of the strong from the weak, the reactors from the perceivers. Norbert Wiener would be delighted at current examples of human thermostats and their behavior. Never before has man been so controllable and easily programmed while foolishly considering himself more sophisticated than at any time in his development.

2) Avoid popular amusements. Take a lesson from the ostrich, whose head-in-the-sand attitude has been universally ridiculed. If timeliness is an essential ingredient of demoralization, existentialism is a perfect vehicle. "Live for today — don't think about the past or the future" has been misapplied to "Dwell on today." We must all respond to imminent situations. We either benefit from, cope with, or succumb to them. But don't go out of your way to encounter any potential problem or worry if you

need not. Don't socialize with those who do, either. They'll bring you down. TV is not the "entertainment" medium it is assumed to be. Newspapers and periodicals aren't either. Pop music is "concerned" music, with lyrics and harmonies unconsciously gauged to the now. Films and plays are simply variants of TV fare. Even the clothes on your back integrate you into the herd unconsciously, if they are "stylish". Stop and consider if whatever you buy, see, listen to, or do is popular. If it is, it is programmed, and like it or not, so are you. Does all this imply that you stop all activity just because it's popular? You figure that one out. It should come easily to a Satanist.

3) Break out of the D.P. time/space warp by realistically and minimally dealing with the present, and dwelling on the past and future. If you need to play the intrigue or crisis game, look back on past scandals and outrages. Patronize that which is out of vogue or not yet in vogue. Seek out persons who are not harbingers of present mores. Discover and share pastimes unrelated to current phobias. Surround yourself with reminders of another social climate and contemplate them as you would a crystal ball. The trend towards nostalgia is an understandable rebellion against the D.P.'s. Its only flaw is that it too has become fashionable and only softens the impact of hardcore downers, which occupy prime-time in our present lives. Reflect, instead, upon personally gratifying things and situations, rather than those labeled "nostalgia" or "collector's edition."

Yes, I realize how tough things have been for many of you this year, for in any such softening up process very few are unaffected. Out of the chaos, the rough beast which slouched towards Bethlehem to be born in the Year One is learning to stand, to walk anew, and His footfalls are creating random upheaval. The Tenth Key has manifested itself in the rolling thunder which has darkened the sky for Satanist and non-Satanist alike. It is for Satanists to know the whys and wherefores of their sorrows. And realizing that, like all their kin — Cain, Prometheus, Orpheus, Frankenstein — they ... *We* ... are, in part or in whole, responsible for our own problems and those of the multitudes. An overview is essential to survival, and what has been sown will soon be reaped. The roses in the garden east of Eden will have thorns. Whatever the blossom, whatever the harvest, the future belongs to us.

Rege Satanas!

On the Importance of Being Evil

VOLUMES HAVE CHARTED THE HISTORY OF MAN'S CRUELTY AND TYRANNY. HOW many have considered the essential role of villainy in human development?

An impartial survey would no doubt qualify the villain as unsung hero. While fusty religionists still cast Satanists in the old, convenient mold, the readily obtainable literature of contemporary Satanism has inspired change in religious thought. Can we expect such an admission by modern theologians? Of course not. It is always a villain, however, who becomes the catalyst for change.

Consider these still fresh examples: If Aleister Crowley had not been "the world's wickedest man," the likes of Gerald Gardner and Margaret Murray could not have stepped onstage for purposes of "enlightenment," and Dennis Wheatley might be a starving hack. They owe their identities to Crowley's outrages. If the Hell's Angels had not caused such a furor, and had not been ritualized in motion pictures like *The Wild One* and *Scorpio Rising*, a "clean, wholesome" interest in motorcycling (and its billions in profits) would not have evolved. The glamour of evil, not fun in the sun, secretly spawned the present bike movement. Pollution reduction, economical transportation — all other rationales for motorcycling are piety devices. If the late Senator Joseph McCarthy had not performed his *auto-da-fe* there would be no movement of the "Politically Correct." If Hitler had not singled out the Jews for discrimination, the nation of Israel might never have been realized.

For every Charlie Manson there are a million solid citizens who can bristle with righteous indignation over his crimes. The same fine folks who stand idly by while a little old lady is being mugged in broad daylight, not wanting to "get involved," invariably alleviate their cowardice by hollering their heads off for stronger legislation against crime. Remember, there is no misfortune so great that somebody else can't put up with it.

A villain is said to be bad, but an apathetic drone is far worse. A villain must be stigmatized so that his opponents can be considered heroic. These heroes are simply reactors who implement a change in affairs sometimes mistaken for "progress." What sets human reaction in motion? A force which is either intrinsically or contrivedly considered "evil."

In order for evil to serve an admirable purpose, it must have method. The lowest level would-be Satanist who thinks he is justifying his existence by committing "evil" acts is the most deluded of all. As has been amply proven, Deep South renegades like Huey Long and George Wallace — certainly considered evil by many — nevertheless exerted reaction on a large scale. The creep whose "evil" deed for the day consists of pulling the wings off a butterfly invariably causes no productive reaction. He cannot rightly be considered evil. Simply moronic.

The more grandiose the villain, the more beneficent he is to society. The small-time villain affects only the microcosm in which he operates, unless his act of villainy is considered so heinous that it spreads beyond his normal sphere of influence. When a villain attains universality, he is endowed with the mantle of devildom. However, if a real villain does not come forward to serve as a convenient embodiment of evil — thereby serving the goodguy's cause — such a person must be developed and sometimes invented.

If evil were by chance eradicated, the race would die of inertia ... at least under existing standards of mental and emotional development. That the villain is the most formidable enemy of boredom was proven in a rather quaint manner by a short-lived tabloid called *Good News*. Feeling that the populace was weary of the standard journalistic fare of murder, rape, war, riot, scandal and catastrophe, *Good News* printed just that — good news. It valiantly lasted two or three issues before its not untimely demise. Why did it die? Good news is only really good to those directly involved. Most people lead such futile and useless lives that only bad news makes them feel better. If not better, certainly gooder. If one cannot gain recognition for anything else, he can rest well with the assurance that he is "good," which in most cases equates with "right". Were it not for an evil to rail against he might just as well never have been born. Yes, Evil is the great savior and sustainer of those who condemn it most.

Duck-billed Platitudes

The rich get richer and the poor get poorer.

The rich do get richer, but the poor, having little or nothing to lose, can only get richer. If diligence will not do it, then charity will.

※

All the world loves a lover.

Bosses hate lovers because they can't keep their minds on their work. The loveless hate lovers because they are envious. Even lovers have little patience with other lovers. They consider another's choice of love object inferior to their own.

※

The best things in life are free.

They may be free for you, but somebody else is paying for them.

※

Honesty is the best policy.

Should read, "Credibility is the best policy."

※

Beauty is only skin deep.

A balm for the ugly, who cannot help but harbor hostility because of their condition. The plain and ugly often mask hostility behind an unctuous or affable facade which is sometimes mistaken for "inner beauty."

※

If at first you don't succeed, try and try again.

A sure way of making a pest of yourself. Better: "If at first you don't succeed, wait and see what happens. If nothing happens, try a different approach. If still unsuccessful, try someone or somewhere else."

※

There is no substitute for hard work.

If you are what others expect of you, it matters not how much or how little you do.

✳

The Goodguy Badge

MAN IS A SELFISH CREATURE. EVERYTHING IN LIFE IS A SELFISH ACT. MAN IS
not concerned with helping others, yet he wants others to believe he is.
Inasmuch as selfishness is akin to pride, and vanity considered the
Devil's work, the first rule of the prideful is to make an exhibition of
piety and charity, with a Goodguy Badge to pin to his lapel.

Man cannot progress one step further towards his own godhood
until he removes that Goodguy Badge.

Mankind's true saviors are not those who led exemplary lives, but
those who have enabled man to pose as Good. Through the cause he
provided against himself, Hitler enables countless millions to become
righteous. Any semblance of goodness detected in moral enemies seems
to dull the luster of the Goodguy Badge. Goodguy Saints are often only
winners in abstinence contests. Perceptive scholars and objective students of human nature aver that most of history's saints have surrepti-
tiously indulged in life's rewards while offering another public picture to
the naïve and conditioned multitude. Leopold von Sacher-Masoch had
not yet written *Venus in Furs,* yet religious and secular Severins were a
zloty a dozen.

The Devil, aside from being the best friend the Church has ever had,
also bestows upon the individual his mantle of Goodness. In whatever
allegory the Devil is conjured, he becomes the reaction device for those
who need him the most. Intrinsically evil people are often hypocrites
who make a show of their Goodguy Badge; without an enemy to plague
them they could never in any believable sense become Good.

This is not to say that one should not be angered at an injustice or
speak out against whatever violates one's security. That is the first law,
the law of self-preservation. But we must consider the motives behind
the selection of an enemy. Perhaps nothing more is threatened beyond
the threat of not having an enemy.

If, having a pain, you inflict sufficient torment to another area of your body it is easy to pretend that the original pain was never there. The Goodguy needs a bad guy to ease the pain of his own inadequacy. This is why his enemy will never perish, for if he did it would bring about great internal pain. Without a cause to take his mind off his own wretchedness he would be lost.

For the bored and simple, those of little or no accomplishment, those who care little whether they live or die, an enemy is essential. Their validity as human beings is measured not by what they can do or who they are, but by who they are against! Paradoxically, these are the hypocrites who shun any manifestations of "negative" propensities. Their vocabularies are turgid with terms like "true," "charitable," "integrity," "spiritual," "equality," "Humanity," "moral," "ethical," "rehabilitate," "understand," "empathy," etc. ad infinitum. Some of these Goodguys, like the fellow who wants to put pants on dogs, are rather transparent. The majority are not.

My purpose here is to make hitherto undetectable Goodguys as visible as Freud made the lady with the closet full of frankfurters. When self-appointed Goodguys are not only spotted but ridiculed for the ostentation of their badges, man will have come a big step closer to the accurate evaluation of personality.

The paramount need to believe in something — anything — has been definitively explained by psychologists Mortimer Ostow and Ben-Ami Sharfstein (*The Need to Believe*, New York: International Universities Press, Inc., 1954). One need not believe in a set of religious principles; if one's faith in a lump of mud is sustenance enough, well and good. If, however, a set of religious tenets is weighty with contrasts between "good" and "evil," the adherent's pietistic requirements must be addressed. Those who wish to gain acceptance from so-called "respectable" people must be Good. Their self-righteousness must be telegraphed in subtle ways, however. It isn't enough to greet everyone with a cheery, "Hello, I-am-a-good-person-so-you-must-accept-me," but by wearing one of the many available Goodguy Badges.

Every peer group has its own Goodguy Badge. The genuinely worthy gain it through individual strength of personality and accomplishment. The rest attempt to gain it by attaching a label to themselves. Psychologists call this "identity." Man either establishes his identity through self or through a collective phenomenon often referred to as a "cause." Celebrities will often use a "worthy cause" to bolster a shaky identity which may have been originally built on individual ability. Public figures simply wear a Goodguy Badge out of pragmatism. It is clear — or should be — that the Great Man is doing absolutely nothing of a genuinely charitable nature.

Although it is a truism that every act is a selfish act, not all are harmful and some are even beneficial to others. Goodguy Badges exhibit tendencies which are often harmful and usually devoid of tangible justification for their existence. Rational self-interest is a virtue, but should be seen for what it is: self-interest. That is the predominant theme of Satanism. Irrational self-interest and undeserved self-righteousness are, on the other hand, hallmarks of the Goodguy Badge.

Religion, having created billions of "undeserving" or "unworthy" followers, is the number one wholesaler of Goodguy Badges. Christian doctrine has become outmoded and unbelievable, even to the most feebleminded. One wonders, "How is it possible for people to be so stupid as to believe the lies they are taught by ministers and priests?" Could it be that among the psychological crutches that Christian dogma has provided, the most obvious is the easiest to overlook? Beyond its horrors and personal repressions, Christianity provides an ingredient essential to the masses' emotional equilibrium: the Goodguy Badge.

The old carnival fortunetellers call a similar ploy "casing the mark" — sending a client away with more problems than when he arrived, the fortuneteller makes him feel glad that he arrived in time. New Age "psychics," on the other hand, simply betray the diminishing quantity of self-aware fortunetellers. In believing their own bullshit they don conspicuous Goodguy Badges, as do the other assorted seers, prophets, channelers and healers who have "received their gift from God." They are applying religious trappings just as surely as did their hair-shirted Anchorite ancestors, and strive for similar sainthood.

The Goodguys are everywhere. Turn on the TV. Within ten minutes a commercial will dramatize the pleas of one of a thousand "non-profit" charities; such charities are spark plugs of the nation's economy. It's easy to see why. The donor Goodguy saves tax dollars. The recipient charity spends ninety percent of the money on "overhead." Management draws inflated salaries and receives kickback tribute from vendors, who in turn are given dispensation to swell up with pride because of their Goodguy affiliation. If the donor donates his money directly to the government instead of a charity, his status would change from Goodguy to taxpaying boob, and such a demotion would cost him more in the bargain. He would have to be crazy not to choose the Goodguy route.

If the Goodguy donates time instead, that's all right too. They assist the charities by justifying the cost of building facilities and the spending of operational expenses.

English nobility are at times forced to maintain their ancestral castles by conducting guided tours, complete in some cases with ghost noises and rattling chains. Nothing so fey in America. The palaces of the once immensely wealthy are being converted into "foundations." In many instances the original families stay put, simply yielding a few rooms to volunteers. In other cases the foundation receives the property lock, stock and barrel, taking the distressed owner off the back-tax hook. The former owner becomes a Goodguy, retiring with his Goodguy funds to a new high-rise or condominium. Chances are good that he was glad to be rid of his white elephant where he rattled about for years with one or two surly servants. He has reached the point where he wants the very thing that his wealth alone may have neglected to bring: recognition. While he's still breathing, he can donate his great paintings to a museum's wing that bears his namesake and bask in Goodguy glory.

Charities solicit those known to have an overabundance not because they can afford to give more, but because they know if the "philanthropist" does not give, he will be depicted as a human monster. Charities choose slogans like, "You can't afford not to give," implying that those who refuse them will receive some sort of retribution for their miserliness. The trick of playing up acts of generosity from those who can scarcely afford to plays on the guilt of those who can.

Mail-order evangelists have been known to bulkmail solicitation brochures depicting a bunch of bloated-bellied "orphans" standing in from of their foundation's "buildings" in Guatemala or Biafra or New Delhi. Investigation might reveal that the foundation's masonite sign covered "New Era Export Co., Ltd." and those kids' faces beamed not for the Lord's blessing but for the quarter's worth of legal tender promised them for posing.

Goodguy causes provide unlimited opportunity for hanky-panky, and not just of the fiduciary variety. If a volunteer of sterling moral propensities meets another equally proper (and equally married) co-worker under physically stimulating conditions, a merger might take place in the supply room one night. A rationale will be available, of course: both parties share a common goal. Charities are as much an opportunity for social contact as the most blatant singles club or dance course, but allow the joiner to be a Goodguy instead of a wallflower or creep.

Who could not find it admirable to want to save humanity? And animals and trees in addition? Or, Satan defend us, the desire to save the world? Actually, the madman who thinks in terms of ruling the world and the equally daft individual who wants to save it are usually one and the same: those who wish to rule the world usually go about attaining their goal in the guise of saving it.

Power-mad Goodguys sublimate these desires by trying to help rule through warfare or help save it through egalitarian politics. These helpers can wear their Goodguy badge without taking on the responsibilities or liabilities of a figurehead. A Goodguy who helps to save the world in the guise of an ecologist simply becomes a microcosmic god serving a macrocosmic client.

It seems to me that the people who holler the most about ecology are the least capable of actually contributing to the planet's development. Quite obviously, the first place to start is to eliminate the source of the problem. The problem of course is people. Get rid of people and you will be rid of the problems they so desire to eliminate.

The armchair liberals who speak reverently of ecological duty would be horrified to implement the totalitarian requirements of compulsory birth control. They shout, "Power to the people!" Power to do what? Make a bigger mess?

Where are all the little men with big ideas? There goes one now, pedaling by the luxury car showroom on his mountain bike, beads of sweat decorating his forehead like translucent jewels. Here comes another putting by in his sub-compact. Neither has any more self-awareness now than they did decades ago when they tooled along in their 300 horsepower monsters. The man on the bike is wealthy. The one in the small car is not. Mr. Cyclist rides one of his Goodguy Badges and gets healthier in the bargain. Little man in little car rides in one of his Goodguy badges and can actually afford to maintain it.

Turn back the clock and listen to another kind of logic. Nobody would buy a small car because it was unsafe, embarrassing and unheard-of. Only youths and eccentrics rode bicycles. Youths because they weren't old enough to drive, and eccentrics because it was healthy — but anyone who was a health faddist had to be a nut.

Are we to assume that man is the only living organism that cannot adjust to its environment? If bugs actually thrive on the pesticides that once fell them, will man's body not accept pollutants, chemical preservatives, etc., as another development of his "natural" evolution? Why are the most sickly-looking people the ones usually seen emerging from health food stores? Could it be that their stringent dietary habits fail to immunize them from "poisonous" foods they are on occasion likely to ingest?

If ecology Goodguys want to practice what they preach, let them establish colonies in undeveloped areas and maintain them with as little contact as possible with the outside world. A few actually have done so, and they are to be admired. They are creating a society from an undeveloped environment. But they will find one thing lacking in their new environment, however. It is the most important ingredient of all in the life of the Goodguy, the lack of which makes his badge meaningless. That missing ingredient is an audience.

I will tell you a story. There was a hermit who lived in a deep wood near a small town. Once each year, on the first day of May, he would stand at the wood's edge for a little while. Then he would go back in the woods, not to be seen again for exactly one year.

He had done this for 20 years, and the only reason he was ever seen was because the children held a maypole dance in the clearing at the edge of the wood. After the fifth year of regular appearances, he became an institution among the townspeople. In fact, it became a feature of the festivities to gather in wait for the hermit to make his appearance. Soon the hermit became the town's best-known celebrity, solely on the strength of his yearly appearance.

On the 21st year he did not appear. Near panic ensued. A search party was formed and the woods scoured. The hermit was nowhere to be found. The townspeople sadly returned to their homes and stores.

The next day, the hermit came walking down the main street of town. Everyone ran up to him and told him of their concern and how glad they were to see him. They insisted that he stay in town and not return to the woods ever again. They not only took care of him, but elected him mayor.

He was not really a hermit, though, nor had he ever been one. A hermit lives alone, without human contact. That man simply had infinite patience and a responsive audience. He was a good showman who became a politician.

Like some "hermits," all wearers of Goodguy badges need an audience. Just as an evangelist needs an environment of sinners in which to operate, the ecology Goodguy requires a polluted urban area. Despite the obvious abundance of sunshine, fresh air and healthful living, blind men seldom join nudist camps.

The closest thing to unabashed slickerism many rustics can witness is in the evangelist's tent. A "man of God" can fleece unconsciously willing victims even easier than a hustler peddling non-Godly wares. The Goodguy Badge that the evangelist supplies in exchange for his thievery ensures his success. Those with a minimum of guilts will become their own victims, and their few inner demons will become the engine for various excesses and vices. Those whose guilts are greater are more guarded in their actions. They are always looking for someone who will take advantage of them.

I have heard many men and women confess, "I know he (or she) is conning me, but I find it so entertaining I really don't mind." When these people are berated for their lack of discrimination or poor judgment, they invariably become all the more attracted to their exploiters. The sin-killing preacher is the ultimate wolf in sheep's clothing: his followers demand that he be so. Despite the luxury cars, dapper clothes and plush living quarters affected by these types, the clichéd criticisms prompted by these accoutrements rarely discourage the faithful. The more grandiose the crusade, the more satisfied are their customers. The guilty are relieved of their guilts and inhibitions — especially in the more violent forms of religious ecstasy.

What, it will be asked, is so terrible about such an arrangement? Nothing. Nothing but self-deceit. God and Jesus maketh the evil man good, the vicious man kind, the smitten man grateful, the victim happy.

What would happen if those divine names were no longer potent enough to placate the weak and inadequate? What of the future, when deceit and treachery will be as easily read as one's name and address? When victims, however willing, will be seen as they are — victims.

When self-deceit can no longer go unrecognized by others, no one will wish to show himself as a fool. Vehicles for self-deceit will either be employed within one's private chamber or publicly presented as amusements — nothing more.

Ominous prophesies of an elite "thought police" will prove to be unfounded. New findings in character analysis will render everyone a potential thought policeman. It will become as easy to assess another's motivations as it is to tell the color of his eyes. The badge of the Goodguy will be visible in every mannerism, and no amount of affectation or protective plumage will disguise character flaws. And the truly good guy will be seen for his inherent goodness no matter how "evil" his superficial trappings may be.

How refreshing it would be to hear a political candidate say:

"I don't believe in God, but in the protection of citizens' health and safety. I plan on placing my friends in executive positions. I will pocket what funds I can get away with, but see that the rest is spent on necessary social improvements. You will have no voice in my decisions any more than you ever had. You will have to accept my judgment, which you will, so long as you are reasonably comfortable, have freedom of movement and opportunity for advancement. If I succeed in fooling the public, the public will have themselves to blame. For I warn you that I am as crooked as any politician can be. Despite my unsavory profession, I will try to keep all of you as happy as possible."

The Church of Satan, Cosmic Joy Buzzer

IN 1966 THE CHURCH OF SATAN WAS BORN, A WITCH NAMED SYBIL LEAKED ON America, and a placental membrane began thickening over the land which was to be called "the occult movement." Sure, there had been those who sent to a Rosicrucian scribe on the back of a magazine cover for the secrets of man's destiny, attended flying saucer conventions, held hands at spiritualists' "closed circles," and read their daily horoscopes. Dennis Wheatley was a blighty hack who shuddered pudding-faced Englishwomen to sleep in their flats. A renegade named Seabrook wrote about strange doings among werewolves and lady vampires (and, incidentally, whose *Asylum* was the original *Cuckoo's Nest),* and two guys named Symonds and Mannix chronicled, respectively, the exploits of "the wickedest man in the world" and the Hell Fire Club. one could obtain the *Sixth and Seventh Books of Moses* and the *Albertus Magnus* in paper before they were called paperbacks. An old man named Roy Heist made good copy selling "mummy's dust" to witchdoctors. Sure, there was an occult movement before the Year One — a movement like a slumbering wino shifting position in a doorway.

No detailed chronology is required to illustrate the events of the past ten years. Concurrent with the increasingly liberal social climate of the 60s, many former taboos became relaxed. The Dark Side displayed itself in polite society, where beatnik poets and bongo drummers had flourished, where witches and tarot readers held court. To most theologians only a single entity was responsible for everything from prophesy to meditation. No matter how innocuous an esoteric act or voluble its practitioner's disclaimer, the Devil was to blame. "Satan" headed more copy concerning the occult than any other teaser. TV-movie adaptations of classic Gothic ghost stories were pushed as "Satanic." Despite indignant attempts to differentiate witchcraft from Satanism, the public insisted on lumping them together in a willing and eager suspension of disbelief. Despite *curanderas'* murmurings of "God given powers," fundamentalists still denounce them as part of the occult movement and minions of Satan.

The lack of imagination and staying power of the occult movement is showing through the veneer of the incompetents who fill its ranks. As the varnish peels away, the occultist's image has become almost as ridiculous as the bible-thumping evangelist's. The Church of Satan could easily become a psychical Ellis Island of refugees and emigrees from the occult scene. Displaced persons who have lost their covens, 90-day magi weary of pondering the Enochian Keys and Crowleyanity, chasuble queens who couldn't make it in the Catholic Church, woebegone wiccans who find that the Goddess's bosom has run dry, Egyptoids who'd be better off as Shriners or in Laurel and Hardy's *Sons of the Desert,* pyramid sitters who've gained nothing but claustrophobia, Atlanteans who get seasick, UFO-ites who've redefined gravitational law but can't chin themselves, witless wizards, sex-starved witches, destitute diviners, pshort-psyted psychics — all the growing residue of a phenomenon that, because of its very popularity, HAD to lose the magic it purported.

Satan translates to mean "opposite," lest the *Satanic Bible* be forgotten. The essence of Satanism is what tips the balance and starts the pendulum swinging in the other direction. That is why the facts of Satanism are so often harsher than the most Gothic melodrama or speculative science-horror fiction. This actual harshness is registered in the dismay of some new applicants who had been enmeshed in the waning occult scene. Interest in the Church of Satan has never been greater, but I don't kid myself into thinking it's because people are more enlightened than ever before — only more disillusioned and/or bored. Nonetheless, I realize that with the decline in the occult movement as a credible identity factor, we have been blessed with an influx of salvageable human potential from the aforementioned categories, as well as "non-joiners" who had been waiting until the dust settled. Thus, the elitism I envisioned in the beginning has materialized fourfold.

In ten years of existence, the Church of Satan has fueled a philosophical counterculture which could have, if unchecked, thrown the baby out with the bath water. It invoked imaginative permissiveness, rational self-interest, and forced a dying theology into ludicrous last ditch behavior (witchmobiles, papal pronouncements, etc.) or running-scared reinterpretation (suddenly "keeping up with social changes"). It also pumped hordes of creeps up till their newly-discovered godheads developed leaks or just plain busted. The ad sections of *Fate* magazine contain as prolific a source of gifted psychics, institutes of cosmic consciousness, and pushers of awareness as can be found in the contact columns of swingers' tabloids or underground newspapers. Add the parasitic fringe: the "ex"'s who seek recognition as *ex*-witches, *ex*-Satanists, *ex*-orcized, or any other wish-they-could-have-but-couldn't-cut-it types. Yes, the occult movement has provided countless persons with delusions of adequacy.

Why has Satanism succeeded? Because from our earliest literature, through the *Satanic Bible,* we have made no grandiose promises of infallible enlightenment and emphasized that each must be his or her own redeemer. That the extent of one's superiority (if any) is governed by one's human potential. That "Satan" is a representational concept, accepted by each according to his or her needs. That is the way it was in the beginning, that is the way it is now. We have rejected that which becomes faddish while championing the unfashionable. When the "monkey see, monkey do" syndrome appears, even on the Left Hand Path, then we don't. We have utilized the best from the worst and discerned the worst in the best and gained through each. We have defied categorization, confounding labelers, knowing that the one label we bear — Satan — is controversy in itself.

In looking back over a decade, it is easy to isolate each phase of our development. It has been not only rewarding as a lesson in behavioral psychology, but has inadvertently served as what sociologists refer to as an "unfunded research project."

The First Phase, *Emergence,* crystallized the zeitgeist into reality — let loose the knowledge of a Satanic body politic into a ready but dumb-founded social climate.

The Second Phase, *Development,* saw an organizational and institutional expansion as a result of carefully stimulated exploitation attracting a variety of human types from which to distill a Satanic "ideal."

The Third Phase, *Qualification,* provided sufficient elucidation to establish the tenets of contemporary Satanism, contrary to prior or current misinterpretation. *The Satanic Bible, Satanic Rituals,* and *Satanic Witch* might have been conveniently overlooked, but were readily obtainable to any who chose to gain knowledge of our doctrine and methodology. An aura of respectability prevailed — often to a point of overcompensation — to counterbalance inaccurate presumptions by the outside world.

The Fourth Phase, *Control,* encouraged dispersion and the Peter Principle as a means of isolating the "ideal" evaluated from Phase Two. De-institutionalism separated the builders from the dwellers, thus filtering and stratifying what began as an initiatory organization — or persuasion — into a definite social structure.

The Fifth Phase, *Application,* establishes tangible fruition, the beginning of a harvest, so to speak. Techniques, having been developed, can be employed. The Myths of the Twentieth Century are recognizable and exploitable as essential stimuli. Human foibles may be viewed with an understanding towards radical embellishment.

The Ides of March had spent its madness and the equinox produced its climactic. At dusk on the eve of the new Satanic Age, I immersed my razor in the waters of Zamzam and embarked upon a new role. I sometimes wonder, would things have been any different without ceremony? Did a ritualistic catalyst help to convince this Pyrrhonic devil that his destiny was being properly exercised?

Symbolism, ritual, ceremony, totem and taboo will always exist and develop or wane as conditions dictate. As Satanists you must perceive such things and having perceived, select or reject in accordance with your needs. Countercultures invariably wind up as dominant cultures. When the occult (hidden) becomes fashionable, it is no longer occult. Yet there will always be a Dark Side. It is the natural Satanist who will be drawn to the abyss of difference, whether it be abstract or concrete. Those who have tarried these past short years in fixed abstractions can feel the warmth provided by their temporal identities cooling. Frightened, they know not what icons to take up, and are befuddled with devaluated doctrines and constrained by programmed hypotheses. Many will become "Satanists," who would once have shunned the name. Others will continue to eschew the name, yet survive on the by-products of Satanism, as they have unwittingly (or unadmittedly) done in the past. For those who are the lost, the disenfranchised, the bored, the ambivalent, we have prepared a place.

The past decade has been gratifying. I thank all of those who have remained loyal to me through the years and given me the feedback any symbolic leader requires. To those of you who were with me in the beginning when the show got on the road, and to you who have since become a part of us in mind, body, or out of just plain orneriness, I am grateful for your support. "Evil" is still "Live" spelled backwards, and if evil we be live we will! Living well is still the best revenge against all adversity. Love, laugh, fancy, create, innovate, reap and revel — as Satanists — in this best of all worlds, World without end. Remember, the first 99 years are always the toughest.

Rege Satanas!

By Any Other Name

MANY ARE THOSE WHO STUDY THE ART OF THE CHILDREN OF DARKNESS, WHO call themselves by the names of witch and warlock, who gaze at crystals, read the tarot, divine by divers means, and seek success through paths of magic. All these play at the Devil's game and take the Devil's tools in their quest for crumbs of power.

In the name of all who suffered and died as the agents of the Devil in ages past, the present band of heretics — those who would deny the Devil, yet play His game — must be called to task. Greater is their folly than the strictest Protestant, Catholic, Jew, or Buddhist. More cowardly are they than the whining informer who plucked at the sleeve of the inquisitor. More flagrant is their hypocrisy than he who reads pornography "in order to warn others."

These are the pursuers of dubious power, the searchers for riches, the buyers of "hidden secrets," the purchasers of "short cuts," the sniveling army of the have-nots who feel themselves deserving of the bounties of life but have found no miracles in the churches in which they prayed.

So now we see them as they swarm about us, purchasing the journals of deceit, the source-books of diabolical supplies, the catalogues of the magical art. They read, and read, and contemplate, and read some more. They study the rites of Lucifer and the mysteries of creation and the spells and charms, and they call themselves by innocuous names. And they play at the games which caused our forebears to be tortured as agents of Satan.

And what do they do, now that it is safe and clear to use His Great Infernal Name? They deny Him! They have the opportunity to take up the very creed of defamation which killed their brothers and sisters of the past and cast that creed before the world in triumphal mockery of its age of unreason. But no — they do not thrust the bifid barb of Satan aloft and shout: "He has triumphed! Rege Satanas!" His art and works which brought men to the rack and thumbscrew, can now be learned in safety. But no ... He is denied. Denied by those who cry up His art and ply His work.

In the safety of their flimsy dens they say the calls. In the warmth of their parlors they push their planchettes and read the cards and cast the runes and call forth the dead and even wear the horns. Seldom in these places is Satan found. For these are the frightened mystics of the new Christianity, and the trembling cowards scurry 'round the openings to the Grottoes of Hell. And like vermin, they furtively nibble upon the newly-emerged Devil-wisdom. Little do they realize the folly of their cowardice.

Ages come and ages go, and cycles reverse themselves with the wondrous periodicity that only nature can sustain, and now we walk upon the upper world.

Those who play the game of self-denial in its traditionally simplistic forms, and showed themselves consistent in their Christ-mongering can find absolution from their sins within our fold.

But those who play the Devil's Game yet cloak themselves in RIGHTEOUSNESS besmirch the names of those who bore the mark of brand and tongs and gazed upon their dead and dying with curses softly spoken. Knew they not, the tortured, that one day men would ply the Devil's handiwork; the work that was grounds for rack and cradle.

Knew they not, the Knights of the Temple, that one day men would fashion spells in the clear moonlight, free from the snare of the heretic-hook; yet deny and denounce the benediction of Satan!

The tongs have gathered rust, and the racks snarl as they turn from lack of oiling. The morningstars have dust between their spikes and the iron maiden is cold and yearning for a lover to embrace.

The ghosts of the Devil-bought will take up the instruments of their destruction and march forth. And their prey will be those scavengers of the arts which once meant Devil-wisdom, and to this day remain as such.

Let it be known that every man who delves into the arts of darkness must give the Devil and His children the due their years of infamy deserve. Satan's Name will not be denied! Let no man shun or mock His Name who plays His winning game or despair, depletion, and destruction await!

The Combination Lock Principle

MAGIC IS LIKE A COMBINATION LOCK. IF EACH TUMBLER FALLS INTO PLACE, THE lock will open. Seldom are any two locks the same. Their physical appearance might be identical, but the combination of numbers necessary to open each is different.

So it is with both individual magical workings and those who attempt them. Goals may appear identical in nature, and magicians similar in training and outward characteristics, but there any similarity stops.

No one can teach another a combination that is his own, for it would not work. Each person possesses his own inclinations, his own Gestalt, and so he must ascertain what works best for him. There is nothing intrinsically esoteric about any combination which will lead to an ultimately successful working unless one considers the *keeping* of the secret combination esoteric, for it is literally that. If the truth is to be known, Greater (ceremonial) magic is simply a means of formalizing acts which in and of themselves would elicit no attention were they to be carried out without ritualistic trappings. Hence a ritual chamber is necessary to make the practitioner feel like a magician, intensifying awareness of his own potential (if any exists). Once one understands his potential, reinforcement supplied by the trappings of a ritual chamber can be superfluous. It's only then when one can get down to brass tacks: the Combination.

Spatial concepts contribute three dimensions to the Combination. The fourth dimension exists in time. If the other three dimensions are placed in correct combination, then the fourth may be obtained. All "supernatural" phenomena occur within the fourth dimension, hence in each instance the spatial or physical boundaries of three dimensions must be present in suitable combination to effect said phenomena.

Every occurrence happens somewhere. It is that "somewhere," in combination with the magician serving as a catalyst, which makes the untoward occur. "Somewheres" need not be specialized enclosures in the obvious sense, but can be fields, cliffs, streets, woods and rivers, as well as structures.

Just as a rainbow is composed of harmonics of light, it is "somewhere" relative to our vantage point; though were we to enter into its apparent field, it would no longer visibly exist. The only way to see a rainbow is from afar — yet it still exists. The fable of the rainbow, with its pot of gold waiting at its base, is the story of man's delusion and disappointment. The magician must realize that his search does not end at the base of the rainbow — he must bypass it for the "somewhere" over the rainbow. There are no curricula for such a search. The combination needed for a controlled working might place the magician not only in diverse places, but in diverse positions and acts. He might need to read a certain book at a certain time in a certain place. Each acts to drop a tumbler in the combination lock.

How does one go about discovering these combinations? One doesn't. They discover him if he is responsive to their appearance. Sensitivity is essential. The harder one looks, the less he will find. "Seek and ye shall find" is a platitude as half-truthful as "the truth will make you free." One can seek until he drops and pass up the answers many times if he hasn't the sensitivity to recognize them when confronted by them. The "truth" can be screamed from a thousand rooftops, and unless it is convenient to hear it will fall on deaf ears.

The most profound acts of magic just seem to "happen." That is because the sets of circumstances which bring them about go unrecognized. Recognition is the key. How can one recognize such combinations when blind to even the most obvious motivations and actions? Or threatened by the accomplishments of another, when one's ego must be strong and secure to become a mage?

Choosing not to recognize is good practice for letting important things pass you by. Peace of mind might be attained, but accomplishment will be missing. If one's ultimate peace of mind rests upon the fulfillment of certain goals, the peace of mind accrued by desensitivity to the obvious is tragically fleeting. The ultimate letdown, which is bound to occur, will make one even more prone to ignorance. Then, contradictory though it may seem, ignorance will become one's sole intellectual and emotional salvation. Parallels in the foregoing statement, as related to organized religion, should be amply evident.

Ravings From Tartarus

PROBABLY THE MOST OFT-ASKED QUESTION I RECEIVE FROM PRACTITIONERS OF Satanic magic is, "Why doesn't my ritual seem to have any effect?"

My answer to this question is invariably, "Because it matters so much to you." Once a ritual has been properly performed, it should not matter much whether or not you see results, for you have supposedly attained — through surrogate means — your original intent. Having "gotten it out of your system" should free you from further concern. This can be likened to an ambivalent feeling towards sex immediately following an exhausting and rewarding sexual experience.

The surest way of succeeding in cursing an enemy is to find a new and equally questionable enemy immediately following the curse you have thrown at your first enemy. If you are inclined towards making enemies, this should present no problem. If not, there are hordes of reprehensible people walking the streets in any community. As potential enemies go, the supply far exceeds the demand.

Stasis is always a deterrent to magical success insofar as dwelling on the object of your working is concerned. Always move on. Never dwell on your desire in dragged-out bits and pieces. Ritualize it out of your system, even if it means isolating yourself in obsessive and painful seclusion. Burn every bit of desire out of your system, and then, when you no longer care, it will come to you.

How can one avoid caring? There are many tricks which can be employed. Creativity is one. When you are in the process of creating something your brain must function on a creative level, not on a rote or repetitive one. Your mind cannot be possessed by one thing and yet entertain new thoughts — unless the object of your creation happens to be in the likeness of your obsession. Here we find an ideal combination, for if the hands can create a facsimile of the desired objective with such dexterity as to be convincing then it is as good as done.

If this method is employed, it follows that the original need is no longer of serious consequence, for your creation has sated your desire. Thus you no longer require what your ritual was originally intended to produce. To oversimplify (though I do not advocate such action): If you want money and cannot get it and you create an approximation of money — sometimes called counterfeiting — the material rewards received could well equal those you would get had you acquired real money. Your need for the real thing no longer matters.

Epicurean masturbation is a perfect example of this theory. Once one's ego flaws have been overcome, it may be realized that an artificial fantasy is infinitely superior to a lousy lay. Yet how often we observe the eternal sexual chase temporarily cease with an "any, old port in a storm" partner. Further frustration ensues.

Them that has gets. Until one has he'll never get. And you don't get it by taking someone else's either. You create your own. If you can't figure that one out, you're not much of a magician.

We all know the reason white witches' curses bounce back. If these crones are consumed with enough guilt to call themselves "white witches" their dastardly act of cursing is indeed threefold guilt-producing — thereby ensuring the backfire of their curses. Here again we observe a static situation engendered by constant re-internalization of the problem for which the rite was performed. Have you noticed how white witches — whether "Traditional," "Gardnerian", etc. — are perennially raising "issues?" Their morass of secular dissension is tempered by the blessed fact that a common enemy exists — the Satanist.

The fact that we have not gone out of our way to stress a difference between witchcraft and Satanism — seemingly their favorite topic — indicates our emancipation from the need for what Thomas Szasz terms "the Other." Satanically speaking, whatever it is we're for it — because "It" is the harbinger of reaction. Magically speaking however, we must take Groucho Marx's stand in the film *Horse Feathers,* where as Professor Quincy Adams Wagstaff, he sings his nihilistic credo, "Whatever it is, I'm against it!"

In this sense we accept "It" (mediocrity, fashion, the status quo, etc.) as a fulcrum point from which to launch the pendulum in the opposite (Satanic) direction. Thus we realize that "issues" — human ideals that they are — are not only transitory but easily predictable.

The Importance of Keeping a Secret

SECRETS ARE POWER. WHEN YOU DIVULGE A SECRET, YOU BARTER THE POTENTIAL power of your hidden knowledge for the fleeting ego boost that comes with its revelation. It is a natural urge to want to impress others by disclosing something thought to be of value, especially when self-esteem is weak or waning. The disclosure is made to one up someone else.

There are four kinds of secrets. The first kind assures the teller of its continued application without giving the game away. A renowned concert pianist can reveal, with relative security, secrets of his keyboard technique to a man who has never touched a piano.

If the same pianist confides an escapade in the bushes with a nine-year-old boy, however, the most unaccomplished acquaintance suddenly has power over him. The latter revelation is the second type of secret, the "skeleton in the closet" secret which often enables one to wield power over another, regardless of social, mental, or economic differences. Employed for financial gain, it constitutes extortion. Wielded as a means of control, it is merely vampiric ego-sustenance.

Unfortunately, a guarded principle is often usable by persons of scant accomplishment, hence the stringent security maintained by innovators and inventors. This is the third type of secret. Unlike the second variety, the revelation of which can undermine the stature of the teller, the third will allow any novice to duplicate that which was formerly limited to the savant. The guy who finds he can double his car's mileage by dropping an inexpensive capsule in his gas tank is a classic example. Such procedures are invariably discovered rather than imparted. A simple formula is far less likely to be revealed than a complex one. But the simplest formulas are usually the most elusive.

The fourth variety of secret is that employed in interrogation and espionage techniques; the "revealing" of a useless piece of information in order to elicit a valid disclosure. In other words, an exchange of a worthless item for a genuine one.

To sum up the foregoing: The first type of secret is safe to reveal, but better to conceal. The second type is certain to undermine its subject by its telling. The third variety will allow the receiver to duplicate what the teller has done. The fourth is a trick of lesser or manipulative magic, preying upon a prurient or larcenous nature.

The holder of a valid secret possesses a tangible and viable commodity and therefore wields the upper hand over those who lack his knowledge. Awareness of this treasure gives him confidence and strength that will project to others. Even if he does not employ the secret, its ready accessibility contributes to his security. Children soon find that they can elicit attention (and candy) from other children by announcing, "I've got a secret."

Some Means of Ensuring that a Secret Will be Kept

1) *Fear:* The threat of dire consequences, should the secret be revealed is the most common means. A fine method, except for many people laws are made to be broken and secrets meant to be divulged. A self-destructive person will find a fertile playground for his masochistic tendencies by revealing secrets, for he places himself in a precarious position for retribution from others. He induces both hostility and rejection while receiving the ego gratification that accompanies a grand exposé. He positions himself as a hero, thus qualifying his potential punishment as martyrdom. I have observed this type of behavior in nuns who run away from a convent only to look forward to penance imposed upon them once they return. Hysterics have joined the Church of Satan, defected, revealed what they supposed to be secrets, and tremblingly waited for a closed limousine to abduct them and bring them to a secret lair where they might be made to endure fierce and delicious punishments.

Fear of retribution alone is probably the least effective deterrent. The oaths taken at fraternal and occult initiations implying that the candidate will be torn asunder should he divulge secrets are virtually worthless since it is assumed such mayhem will not actually occur. The more upstanding and respectable an organization, the less validity such oaths present. Fraternal orders usually depend upon the next category, despite their bloodthirsty oaths.

2) *Ostracism:* Ostracism is a very real threat. To work, the keeper of a secret must place no small amount of dependency upon the fellow-ship his comrades provide. Fraternal groups employ this deterrent, especially in communities where ostracism can mean business loss in addition to social rejection.

Some secret orders impose a sort of "statute of limitation" as a result of indiscretions. This means that if the candidate's trustworthiness is found lacking, he will find himself limited to a lower peer group where classified material is not known. Once it has become general knowledge that such a separation process exists, anyone with an eye towards advancement will exercise discretion.

The obvious disadvantage of ostracism is that its effectiveness is limited to a social environment. A member might be a paragon of discretion while residing where he is dependent on his brothers for emotional and economic security. Should he move away, with no thought of returning, however, he will often spill the beans to acquire fresh recognition.

3) *Ridicule:* If a secret is far-fetched or padded with asinine antics, many will think twice about revealing it, lest their listeners look down on them for their lunacy. Hence many valid secrets have been surrounded by the trappings of an apparently laughable nature. Many lodge brothers, especially those of a highly businesslike and respectable demeanor, would hesitate to describe rituals wherein they were made to dress up as women, ride a goat, urinate on the floor, lie in coffins, etc. Such antics, within context, have symbolic meaning, but a casual expla-nation somehow guarantees that they will still be taken out of context.

4) *Silence:* The most effective way to ensure secrecy is to not divulge a secret in the first place. The greatest magical secrets are those that, if told, would alienate the listener from the teller. If a magician would respect a student enough to divulge such secrets, he would not wish to alienate him. Consequently, such secrets are never told. They are only discovered. The fact that discovery is a desirable human occurrence ensures its contrived use as a means of exploitation and control.

The Discovery Game

If you want people to wholeheartedly accept what you have to offer, let them "discover" it a la the Easter Egg method. Now, you all remember how the Easter Egg Hunt worked. Somebody got up early — earlier than anyone else — and went out with the eggs that were later to be discovered by the kids. He or she hid them in places where they could be found, but not without a bit of a search.

All the kids could hardly wait to get started. Of course they all arrived at the same location. None of them went to another site, unless they were awfully stupid or misdirected by a scurrilous chum. As each kid discovered an egg, he would holler with joy. Occasionally a parent, upon seeing their offspring's discovery from the sidelines, would holler too. The child who amassed the greatest number of eggs usually received some sort of recognition, often a hollow chocolate bunny.

You know as well as I that those kids couldn't care less about the eggs once they got them home. Pop invariably got them in his lunch box for the next week.

The point is that a false demand can be created where there is absolutely no need for a product, simply by creating an opportunity for discovery.

John Doe finds the opportunity to discover something so attractive because he has not, will not, and could not discover anything on his own in a lifetime. What's worse, a tiny voice inside lets him know it. So when someone comes along who provides an opportunity to ameliorate an inherent lack of perception, the opportunity is seized. If you doubt what you have just read, consider how the Hidden Persuaders employ the magic word "discover." "Discover this new taste treat" cajoles the commercial, and one's unconscious leaps to the lure, the same lure on a nickel and dime level that on a loftier plane drove Ponce de Leon, Sir Richard Burton, Leif Erikson, Columbus, Peary, and the Shadow, who, several years ago in the Orient learned a strange and mysterious secret: the power to cloud men's minds.

Occultism for the Millions

I HAVE ALWAYS HARBORED A NATURAL REPUGNANCE TOWARD FADS. WHEN THE most rewarding and exhilarating interest becomes a fad, its evocative qualities enjoyed by the few are diminished by mass acceptance. This must not be confused with being jaded. To be jaded does not imply that many others are doing the same thing, but that one no longer finds stimulation in it. Often one can become jaded with something, only to later return to it after a passage of time creates the reawakening known as nostalgia.

Occasionally my eyes will light up at hearing or reading about discovery or innovation on the part of someone engaged in the exploration of the unknown. This trait is analogous to true Satanism. For every such Promethean individual, there are a hundred others "proving" their prowess in magic by sitting in pyramids, building orgone cabinets, photographing leaves and tracing Dracula's past. If I hear of a person looking for fairies in his garden, at least I am amused at his singular pursuit, for few seek fairies in their own gardens any longer.

There is nothing wrong with sitting in pyramids or constructing orgone accumulators, any more than eating banana splits or skydiving. But if you fancy yourself a magician, don't flatter yourself on the merits of your investigations. You are neither innovative nor farsighted. Just going along with a fad.

A prime example of occult faddists' chicken-with-a-beak-on-the-line methodology is their tendency to grab up anything that has been set forth as arcane. When Wilhelm Reich was "discovered" by the occult movement, they failed to recognize that, as I stated on the dedication page of *The Satanic Bible,* he knew more than cabinet-making. How many have pursued theories advanced in *The Cancer Biopathy?* Who has attempted to duplicate Reich's "cloudbusting" and to relate it to the rainmaking principles of Charlie Hatfield or aboriginal shamans? Who knows a good case of "character armor" when he sees it? Or has

expanded upon *The Function of the Orgasm?* Because enclosures are all
the rage and occult journals expound their ramifications (so long as they
are pyramidal), Reich's following is largely limited to cabinetmakers.

It's a cinch that if you read it in an occult periodical or paperback,
everyone's doing it. That should be your cue to avoid such stuff, lest
you be relegated to the same readership level. As time proceeds, the
table-tipping of Annie Besant becomes the Kirlian photography of
today. The Ouija board becomes the mind machine unit, complete with
flashing red LEDs and "subliminal" sound. And turbaned East Indian
swamis move aside for "psychic rescue squads." Mediums? Channelers.

It still takes far more practice and skill to type well than to read
auras. Or to change a transmission than to make predictions like, "A
famous singer will have marital difficulties this year." Pop occultism is
fodder for nincompoops, and its only merit is that it detracts from established religious mores. Occult (hidden) knowledge will seldom be
found in obvious sources. The very phrase, "popular occult movement,"
is a contradiction in terms. Satanism cannot rightly qualify as an occult
phenomenon, and I have never claimed it as such.

One's personal delvings can be considered occult in the true sense
of the term only if they remain outside the pale of supernormal faddism.
The would-be innovator asks, "If I cannot find food for thought in
source material akin to my interests, where then?" The answer is found
in the analogy that one does not "find" one's self. One creates one's self.
Magical power is accrued by reading unlikely books, employing unlikely situations, and extracting unlikely ingredients, then utilizing these elements for what would be considered "occult" ends. After one has
observed the results of such creative unions, what was originally considered "unlikely" will be seen as the most easily understandable methodology.

The Blow-Off
or
Kroger Babb, Where Are You Now That We Need You?

FOR CREATING INTRIGUE, AN AMBIGUOUS STATEMENT IS INFINITELY PREFERABLE to the straightforward one. The more intrigue created, the more frantic others become to partake of what you have to offer. For example, as a Satanist, I am sometimes asked about sex orgies by the deeply frustrated. A knowing wink will do more to get them slobbering than any amount of lurid description. It would be senseless to improve upon the explicit vistas provided by modern pornographers.

I'll never forget a man I worked with on a carnival's back lot who ran what was known as a "sex show." Not to be confused with a "girly show," the "sex show" consisted of a tent lined with medical posters ostensibly demonstrating the wonders of the human reproductive system, the ravages of V.D. and the breasts and buttocks of Hottentot women in various stages of development. Behind roped-off sections were exhibits: a waxen two-headed baby (known in the trade as a "pickled punk"), a couple of "medieval" chastity belts (made by a Tucson sheet metal worker), an array of tongs, forceps, catheters, and breast pumps (under glass), a reproduction in wax of a noseless face of an unfortunate syphilitic gentleman, and other educational wonders.

A "doctor" would get the rubes into the tent by appearing on the bally platform with a rather sleazy blonde wench dressed in a nurse's uniform two sizes too small and in need of laundering. With a dented reflector fitted to his forehead and a stethoscope around his neck, the surgical-smocked doctor would blame the microcephalic condition of a pinhead, borrowed here from the sideshow, as a result of improper genetics. The pinhead, standing at the doctor's side, would simper innocently, nodding its little cranium in unknowing agreement. The doctor didn't sell medicine, as one might have expected him to, and proceeded with a far more sophisticated game.

After the customers filed into the tent to view the secrets of mankind and the miracle of life, the magic would really begin. When the ten minute guided tour ended at the last exhibit (the pickled punk, presented with a brief discourse on improper sex education), a dim glow could be seen through a tent flap hung at the extreme rear of the museum, next to where Doc was holding court. Presumably, the light came from his living quarters, where the yokels were inclined to peek through.

While the marks were furtively looking through the lit-up flap, the doctor was beginning his big pitch. Since the audience consisted only of males (which was usually the case), maybe they would like to see first-hand "the modern method of sexual hygiene." In hushed tones, the doc announced that they would be shown practices and things which were to be avoided in order to maintain a sound mind and body.

Those who "chanced" to glance through the tent flap during the Doc's build-up saw the aforementioned dirty nurse reclining on a shabby cot reading a movie magazine, her ample thighs revealed above the tops of her stockings. A small nightstand next to her carried an immense jar of Vaseline. On the wall, directly above the nurse's cot, was pinned a slightly whiter piece of bedsheet, suggesting a motion picture screen. The remaining area was occupied by about twenty folding chairs. A folding card table stood against the tent wall opposite the cot, supporting a scuffed movie projector. From what was glimpsed, this was a show that should not be missed.

The small knot of rubes that had remained to listen/peek were by this time hanging on to the doctor's every word, who announced "limited seating available for the show about to begin in the inner tent." Seats were only an extra 50 cents, but the lecture and demonstration was "only allowed to be shown to serious students of art, anatomy, or medicine."

Perceiving the gleam in the eye of serious students, Doc then made the final pitch before bringing out his roll of tickets. "Well, all I can say fellows, is you're going to see something today that you'll remember as long as you live!" As the words were being spoken, he cautiously bent forward, as if to better observe anyone who might have crept into the tent unnoticed. He then lifted his outstretched middle finger for all to see, and closed his other hand into a sheath which he slid over the projecting finger three or four times, slyly winking as he did so.

No further enticement was required. The doctor couldn't rip the tickets off the roll fast enough. And when the audience finally found themselves seated, the overripe nurse was nowhere to be seen; she was outside on the bally platform with Doc warming up a new crowd while an assistant materialized within the "auditorium."

What the rubes did see was a 16mm movie showing a Caesarean delivery and subsequent incubator care of an infant, followed by a superbly acted Office of War Information produced drama, a tender story of a GI who meets a girl on a furlough, and neglecting to obtain a rubber, contracts a social disease. The fifteen-minute epic ends with five glorious minutes of tight close-ups of oozing chancres, eaten-away palates and running sores.

By the end all unconsumed popcorn, sno-cones and orange drinks had been abandoned under the seats, and at least one rustic lad had fallen ill. None manifested disappointment that the show was over.

The doctor shall remain anonymous, for he now may be practicing in some large hospital. One thing is certain, however: prurience thrives on ambiguity, and the need for mystery in everyone's life demands subtlety, suitably dispensed.

The Whoopie Cushion Shall Rise Again

NOT LONG AGO I WAS TOLD OF AN ENTERPRISE IN NEW YORK CALLED "AGENTS of Pie-Kill Unlimited." That noble venture, whose motto is "Have Pie, Will Travel," specializes, for a fee, in performing edible indignities upon likely candidates. In addition to pie-in-the-face attacks, they render such services as seltzer-water barrages and squirt-gun contracts. Their tactics are in the strict tradition of past experts like the Three Stooges, Laurel and Hardy, and Mack Sennett.

"Pie-Kill" is dedicated, among other things, to the stamping out of pomposity. Which brings me to an important factor — one which practicing Satanists should consider in their world view: comedy.

The twin masks of tragedy and comedy exist as irrevocably as any other duality. Yet it is the mask of tragedy that is worn most often for magical means. Desire for that which is unfulfilled is always a little bit tragic, and those who frequent the ritual chamber most, often lead the most tragic lives. In order to generate an emotional response conducive to a successful working, one cannot easily extract humor. Nor, in most circumstances, should one try.

Frequently humor can serve to alleviate or attain a situation before solemn ritualization becomes relevant or required. Unfortunately for a multitude of occultists, humor is a rare ingredient in their lives. In fact it is their very lack of humor that has impelled them into the arcane and esoteric. Someone once commented to me that a sorcerer without a sense of humor would be intolerable. I agree and will add that, in addition to being intolerable, he would be incompetent.

Candidates for pies-in-the-face are more plentiful than ever. Less messy but equally inhumane indignities are easily implemented. I have an entire trunk full of the weaponry of humiliation, gathered from many places and spanning a 50-year period, 1900-1950 — the golden era of practical trickery.

After 1950, people started getting crazy notions about human dignity, and the practical joke was neglected for the serious protest. The change was needed, but something was lost in the process, as is usually the case. Now fun is poked at institutions rather than at individuals. A sort of collective humor has replaced what was once a personalized pratfall. *Mad* and the *National Lampoon,* entertaining as they are, have provided a like-minded readership with universal victims. The butts of jokes are no longer selected with careful deliberation, but are ridiculed *en masse.*

Purveyors of joke items like Johnson, Smith & Co. no longer send 600-page catalogues to customers, but live on past glories with thin catalogues. A time approaches, though, when seers like Jeanne Dixon will sit upon a #2953. ("The Whoopie Cushion or Poo-Poo Cushion, as it sometimes called, is made of rubber. When the victim unsuspectingly sits upon the cushion, it gives forth noises that can be better imagined than described. By mail postpaid. No. 2953, 25¢.") All is not lost. A host of solemn and humorless victims are being primed for not only "Pie-Kill" but Poo-Poo Cushions, Joy Buzzers, Black-Eye Telescopes, Trombone Nose Blowers, Itching Powder, Rubber Chewing Gum, Dribble Glasses, and Squirting Stickpins.

Too long have curses and anger been wasted on deserving victims whose most devastating insecurities could be brought forth by a harmless practical joke — one which a more secure person would accept with mild annoyance at worst and amusement at best. Those who deserve ridicule have been living in a climate that provides relative immunity while their pomposity has gone unchallenged and even encouraged. Satanists are anathema to the pious, the sanctimonious, and the hypocritical. They should also be the nemeses of the pompous. Satanists — Atten-shun! Right shoulder Whoopie Cushions! To the rear — *harch!*

The Threat of Peace

"EUSTRESS" IS A TERM THAT DESCRIBES AN EMOTIONAL STATE OF FUN-FEAR OR pleasurable discomfort. Although they are antonyms, we shall see how what begins as distress can lead to eustress. Since most people live their lives in a programmed series of distresses and fears, a social environment wherein security and comfort are only present if a certain amount of crisis prevails.

The human mind abhors a vacuum. Wild animals have no such problem. Every cell of their brains functions. Only when domesticated or conditioned is a necessary survival engram replaced by another. Man is the only animal who must be continually reminded of existence. Any sensation will do. In other words, something must happen lest life become not only meaningless but genuinely painful. How many times is the expression heard, "What's happening?" A satori-like Shangri-La existence eagerly sought by many would be unbearable if realized. Not because of the pressures of peace but by the inability of most minds to independently devise enough thoughts to maintain mental stimulation.

Stress has become such a normative — and therefore comfortable — way of life, that it has become necessary to people's existence. A paradox has evolved wherein humans are constantly bombarded by stress situations (which they crave) and then cautioned to reduce their craving. This remarkable sequence can be likened to the weekday sinner who goes to church each Sunday. A conscious attempt at reducing emotional stress amidst a society which fosters habitual stress can only compound frustration.

I have written at length on the hypocrisy of the human race. History and empirical evidence more than bear out any rantings I may add. Part of that great hypocrisy is man's — especially contemporary man's — lip service to "freedom" and human dignity, when in reality his self-awareness is sustained by a series of masochistic maneuverings. This is where distress becomes so commonplace that it represents comfort, security and fun. Such is the evolution of eustress from an otherwise distressful situation.

Blatant examples of this transition are most common in an erotic context. The pleasure/pain factor is the entire basis of sado-masochistic activity. What invariably begins as an unpleasant experiences evolves into eagerly-anticipated gratification. Here we have a basis for eustress phenomena. If a child receives little attention except though punishment, that child begins to court punishment. If punishment is received at the hands of someone who is stimulating, the attention is well worth it.

Substitute that microcosmic situation with a macrocosmic one in an adult world and without any overt sexual connotation. Here's the picture:

A man feels insignificant. There is overpopulation and under-recognition. He is made to feel like a big shot because of his consumer power or a token title which his firm has bestowed upon him. He still feels insignificant. He is married and has a family which he might be able to feel pride in, if less demands were placed upon him which he is either loath or unable to meet. This makes him feel like a jackass. But he sees a guy on a TV show with whom he can identify. He feels a little better while watching the guy on TV or thinking of him. Still, he feels insignificant. He has a few heroes whom he sees on other TV shows: sports figures, a tough cop or a late-night talk show host. He lives vicariously through all of them.

Unbeknownst to himself, he experiences his viciousness vicariously through his "angry" indignation (and unrecognized identification) with the friends and killers he sees on the news. But good or evil, benign or malignant, none of these people are him. They're getting attention. He's not. He feels insignificant. Well, if he feels insignificant, maybe, just maybe, it's because he is.

It's not that he's dumber than some of those getting all the attention. Chances are good some of them are, in their own way, just as programmed as himself. But there's only room for so many to stand in a spotlight, and he's left out.

What does he do? What alternatives are open to him to be able to pinch himself and know he is still there? He can get into some kind of trouble, great or small, and receive attention. The only drawback to that is that he'll have to answer a lot of questions and encounter situations which may be less cope-able than his ennui. The other way is to "get involved" in something — anything — that will grab his emotions enough to qualify his existence. His very own problems are apparently not good enough for full time mind occupancy. They're not serious on a world-shaking level. And nobody he talks to about them gives a shit. But if he burdens himself with common-denominator crises of a local, state, national or international nature, he can find plenty of company, share gripes, make friends (and enemies) and generally feel as though he is All Right.

He has chosen a life of eustress and the safety which accompanies it, in preference to the solitary distress of living a dangerously unprogrammed life. Why is this man's unprogrammed life dangerous? Either because he has problems which are not universal enough to share, or because his mind is such a vacuum that its own resources cannot pull him out of his feeling of insignificance.

Now, somewhere out there exist pretty sharp cookies who know about man's need for eustress, and are more than willing to supply it. Aside from being rather profitable, it masks, through the gifted art of misdirection, what's really happening. Everything is a softening-up process for something else. You have been set up. You are being set up. Someone, somewhere, who is on the take is not missing a trick in the book. You have been conditioned to look in the wrong direction at the wrong things, find great fun in that which you should soberly evaluate, and take very seriously that which should be ridiculed and laughed out of sight and sound.

Getting back to planned problems for entertainment and enjoyment: The soap opera is a masterpiece. Its evolution is concurrent with eustress needs. When women had enough personal headaches in an epoch where "women's work is never done," childbirth deaths and suicides over being "compromised" — there were no soap operas. Not that it was right. Simply that no matter how devoid of imagination or how bored a woman may have been able to be, there was no chance of it usurping daily "shit work" requirements. Only the wealthy or spoiled could afford to be bored.

When radio inaugurated the soap opera, the medium became the message (ah, misdirection!) and women who listened while performing their chores were already being processed into a new form of consumerism. The troubles they heard were more interesting (and romantic) than their own, but they were troubles just the same. Hence, another woman's problems became a vicariously glamorous substitute for what could, with luck, be the listener's. The genesis of the soaper is pretty well defined. Now, most who view them neither toil nor spin while doing so, but simply absorb the blissful turmoil and sexy anguish, wide open for the inculcation of the real substance of the show: the products advertised. And the supreme irony is that the viewers prefer to believe that they are more independent and emancipated (like the women on the screen) than ever before.

In the *Satanic Witch's* considerable exploration into the world of eustress, the thrill rides of amusement parks are cited. In the late 1970s, Sociologist Marcello Truzzi participated in a documentary on rollercoasters which was narrated by Vincent Price. Dr. Truzzi's perceptive comments notwithstanding, it was interesting for me to see certain persons on the most "dangerous" rides let go of the safety rail despite repeated warnings. When I worked carnivals and parks, there were always the nuts who let go at the wrong places. Sometimes they would fly out and even get themselves killed. My point is, even though coasters were safety-tested, and eustress the motivating factor in riding, and lawsuits weren't honored if the "ride at your own risk" sign was displayed, the stupid, careless, irresponsible member of society was not protected from himself. Fun-fear with complete safety has helped to foster irresponsibility and devalue life and property.

If I were to build a rollercoaster, it would be shot through with visual and audible warnings to hang on and not stand up while the car is in motion. Anyone failing to comply with the very real warnings would hurl to the ground. Eustress would then turn to distress — the distress of the unexpected.

Curses by the Dozen

YOU HAVE BEEN CURSED. EVERY DAY YOU ARE THE RECIPIENT OF VERY REAL and magically formidable curses. One who is versed in the psychology of hexes generally evaluates them in terms of highly personal attacks, based on real or imagined injustices or slights. In short, you curse another to get revenge, or someone attempts to curse you for the same reason.

In the sending of a curse, it is presumed that a strong degree of emotion must be the motivating factor. If one simply goes about throwing random hexes, supposedly nothing will happen. As the *Satanic Bible* explains, one should really mean it if any form of ritual magic is performed. The same text also states, though, that if you curse someone who is undeserving, nothing will happen. What is the standard of "deserving" — what constitutes a deserving victim? As we know, those qualities are also covered in the *Satanic Bible*.

Assuming someone is not a deserving victim, though, they can be easily modified into a reasonable facsimile. In other words they can be set up to act unreasonably, harbor guilts and fears and generally behave in a manner which will attract disaster and court failure. The reason fortune tellers actually can curse people much of the time is because the seer's clients are "ripe" the moment they walk though the door.

A benign or even tactful fortune teller or psychic will never foretell really bad tidings to a client, because a dire prophecy emanating from a credible source will most likely happen. The fact that a client wants to be told what is about to happen guarantees the reliability of whatever is forecast.

Let's multiply this principle to a high social power, with media the medium and the public as the sitter or client. A public unused to doing its own thinking looks to diverse authorities for guidance, not to mention amusement. The general public is, quite literally Easy Marks, Unlimited. Hence, it is easy to understand why their concerns and fears are prepackaged — and to someone else, profitable to prey upon.

Each day you are bombarded with dire warnings and ill tidings. "No news is good news" is a truism. Good news doesn't sell. More people are working at media-related jobs than ever. It takes "bad news" and emergencies for them to keep their jobs. The more bad news you hear and read, the more depressed you become. Other people's bad news rubs off on you. Problems beget problems. Everywhere you turn, you are reminded of one of the myriad hazards to health, economic stability or domestic tranquility. You are not supposed to be simply aware or prepared for unpleasant contingencies. You are supposed to be scared shitless. It's easy to scoff and say, "I don't let that sort of thing get to me," but like it or not, it does.

Theoretically, people should live longer because of medical advances over the past half-century. With its creature comforts, mass consumerism should have made lives happier. Egalitarian education should have made people smarter and more articulate. Instead, people are feeling sicker, sadder and more tongue-tied than ever.

Contemporary pulpit-pounders blame it all on "a breakdown of moral fiber and relaxing of spiritual values." If there is any value at all in that absurd claim it is that if you are zealously self-righteous enough to be a religious nut, you won't feel any guilt about anything you do: anything you see or hear will be ignored; and you may go about acting like a first-class sonofabitch with immunity. But then, if someone were honest enough to say, "I will plunge headlong into 'spiritual values' just so the hype of the outside world won't get to me," the whole thing would be a contrivance and its effect doomed to failure.

Brainwashing is the only manner by which an individual of average intelligence can be filled with "spiritual value." Those who come by it naturally are of sub-human mentality. This is a brutal, insensitive world and the more it is populated, the greater the diversity of deceits and scams and setups become necessary for human survival. When Barnum declared, "A sucker is born every minute," he hadn't foreseen the Malthusian population increase of a century later.

As I've stated, opportunities for individual expression haven't lessened; there are just more people around. Each, in his or her own way, is scrambling for survival. The Western world is a giant flea market of conflicting interests hawking their wares. Competition is far beyond the point of free enterprise in its conservative sense; and even though you are, by necessity, one of the exploiters, you are also, from someone else's standpoint, a victim.

You may be completely solvent financially with an increasingly successful business, yet cursed by the effects of mass media in other ways. Your family or spouse may be an insurmountable problem. Or you might be worried sick about heart attack, cancer, cystic fibrosis, AIDS, multiple sclerosis, sickle cell anemia, etc. Listen kiddies, the day when family problems were as simple as in-laws, poor school grades, unwed motherhood, reform school and adultery, pale by comparison to the profound traumas suffered now domestically where none should even exist.

The big killers of yesterday were tuberculosis and constipation, the latter being the most hyped. Sure, people died of other things, but weren't hexed into them ahead of time. They used to go crazy from masturbation, it was claimed, and some most likely did — from worry. The medical profession has the power to cure, but its propaganda techniques are flagrant curses.

Christianity still harbors formidable opposition to birth control, yet whines about the plight of neglected children in underdeveloped countries (where missionaries are running the hospitals). "Sponsor a foster child" exhorts a Christian "charity." If they really wanted to do something, they would fight those elements of their own religion who would stifle mandatory birth control. If you haven't guessed by now, the name of the game is Give With One Hand, Take Away With the Other. You are being beaten down by the very thugs who will then come to nurse your wounds.

As Satanists, you are just a tiny step closer to honesty, a wee bit tougher in the will department, and slightly more sensitive as a barometer. In this world of sameness, you are outrageously different just in being a Satanist, and that alone is quite a distinction. The more individuality and freedom from thought-pollution you can retain, the less affected by wholesale hexes you will be.

Hatha Toilet Seat Meditation

THE BEST PLACE TO MEDITATE IS ON THE POT. IF YOU HAVE A COMFORTABLE toilet seat and a stout lock on the door, there's no telling what great thoughts might emerge. Martin Luther dreamed up Protestantism while sitting on the toilet at Wittenburg monastery, and we know what a big movement that became.

There is no place where one is as receptive to outside influences as on the toilet, with immersion in a hot bath second and the shower third. That is why a long-awaited phone call or ring of the doorbell will certainly occur under those conditions. The greater the state of relative helplessness one enters, the greater the receptivity.

Requiring the most privacy, surpassing both bath or shower, the toilet is unexcelled in attracting outside impressions and influences. Those who allow others to witness them in the bathtub, shower, or even engaged in sexual intercourse, will usually draw the line when it comes to receiving audience on the toilet. The toilet is the most sacrosanct vestige of isolation available in an otherwise crowded environment.

Pressure on the vertebrae is relaxed while sitting on the throne, easing both mental and physical tension. Genitals are completely exposed and unhampered by clothing or pressure. If the chamber is sufficiently soundproofed, or outside noise attains sufficient decibel levels, non-verbal utterances may freely proceed in any intensity or pitch, and from any orifice. The infantile release of what we have been conditioned to hold back at all other times provides a psychological as well as physiological catharsis.

With such conducive conditions to relaxation and receptivity, the brain will function more freely and range further afield for informational input. Many do their best reading on the toilet, absorbing input while releasing outflow.

I once knew an elderly hermit, a brilliant scholar who had built a miniature castle in the woods of northern California. Until his retirement, he had operated a large chain of theaters in England. After coming to the U.S., he purchased a small plot of land in the redwoods and single-handedly constructed a fairy tale castle from odds and ends. Tiny gables and filials rose above the stone and wood dwelling, which held four small rooms.

To simplify plumbing and butane installation, he combined his kitchen and toilet facilities, the stove next to the john, with the table on which he dined in front of it. Thus he could sit on the toilet, prepare dinner off to one side, move the completed meal on to the table and sup. Neighbors from the surrounding area spoke derisively of "the dirty hermit," despite being an impeccable dresser and a great intellect. Eventually, the iconoclastic old gent died, his little castle demolished, and a split-level built on its site.

Perhaps he had more than just convenience in mind when he combined his kitchen and toilet. I wonder how many people, if given the opportunity, would like to eat at the same time as eliminating. Caracalla, Diocletian, Nero did just that — and more.

The toilet is more than a throne. It is a sacred chamber. *Vale* Chic Sales.

Custress, Vampires, and Vicariousness

AS I HAVE STATED, THE PARADOX WHERE MORE PEOPLE ARE "TALKING" DARK forces up, down, and sideways, but fewer than ever are actually living as night people, provokes speculation. The moral here is that when everybody's talking, very few are doing. More time is spent comparing notes with aficionados than in enjoying the hobby *per se*.

In a puritanical society filled with the sort of fears and guilts that become a kind of security blanket, real displeasure ensues when there is a confrontation with the truly outré or bizarre. It's fun to be scared, so long as it is safe and predictable. For example, a person can enter a movie theatre and see a horror film (at a reasonable hour, of course — there are hardly any more all-night theatres). After the film ends, no matter how frightening, there is the safety of the exit and "normal" life outside. Amusement parks have always served the same purpose and the roller coaster is designed to allow for "daring" fun-fear. By contrast, the unexpected experience, no matter how trivial, can be terribly unsettling.

Nocturnal non-involvement is largely due to omnipresent vicariousness. It is easier (and presumably safer) to live out nocturnal fantasies through science fiction, gothic romance and the aforementioned spate of horror films. Vicarious outlets abound in every facet of popular culture, be they comic books, music, or parapsychology. Wherever the dark side of human experience can adapt to vicarious expression, the "real thing" will be shelved. It has been observed that those who talk about sex the most, do it the least. It is certain that the same principle applies in other areas.

There is nothing "morally wrong" with vicariousness. Only when it compounds rather than relieves frustration is it harmful to a true individualist. It helps when the vicarious one recognizes his own vicariousness, though no one else need be the wiser. Many of the most esteemed business and professional people have built their entire reputations on carefully disguised vicariousness.

There is a thin line between vicariousness and sublimation. Both are forms of substitution. The vicarious one substitutes another's life for his own — he lives off of someone else's identity. What he cannot or will not be he finds in another person and assumes that role, usually in secret. When he becomes downright imitative, however, he is no longer vicarious, and must sink or swim according to his ability for mimicry. One can't be a wooden duck — then, when the fox is coming, be unable to fly away. We are plagued with an age of "sameness" because so many people are content to imitate a handful of basic types. Hence a shortage of real "characters." A character is not a creature of mediocrity, and even if he is imitative, his mimicry is so outlandish that he becomes a travesty.

In today's society people paradoxically desire safety, anonymity and security on one hand and lust for recognition, applause and individuality on the other. As things have worked out, most live herd-like vicariously pretending to be someone else. The dilemma is not so much in the drone life of the herd but in the limited selection of role models. Any costume party amplifies the last statement. Costume shops will tell you what vicarious role models are always in greater demand than others, when the protective lid is blown off for a masquerade.

The insane are more likely to wear the shoes of their role models heavy-footedly. That's why nut houses are likely havens for Napoleons, Jesus Christs, Hitlers, and in recent years, Lucifers. In between the herd-person and the Napoleons are those who have worked their vicariousness into gratifying sublimation. Have you ever noticed how most plainclothes cops look and act like the ones on TV police shows? Which came first? The answer should be obvious. Oscar Wilde was astute when he proclaimed his famous reversal, "Life follows art." He only went halfway, though. People imitate a life which is an art form, an artificiality, to begin with. In short, they are imitations of a fabrication. Human redundancies.

Sublimation in its purest form is often self-realized. A foot fetishist becomes a shoe salesman; a necrophile, a mortician; a prostitute, a sociologist; a meddler into intimacies, a priest or psychiatrist; a racketeer, a "legitimate" businessman. The list grows quite long. I knew a young guy who was studying to be a mortician many years ago. People always got around to the question, after much verbal detouring, "Why do you want to be a mortician?" The reply was, "Because I like to play with dead bodies." That is what is known as "pulling the rug out from under."

Million d'Arlequin, Vesti la Giubba, et al.

But the theater itself seems to me so puny as against the hourly drama of life itself that for me at least it becomes an anticlimax. — Gene Fowler

IT HAS OFTEN BEEN SAID, "THE WORLD'S A STAGE, AND WE'RE ALL ACTORS." Interpreted in its most ego-gratifying way, this maxim closely rivals Ipsissimus Crowley's "Every man and woman is a star." Reality, however, like the theater, is far less democratic in its central casting office.

The world *is* a stage, but few qualify as bonafide actors. Most are spearcarriers, supporting players — in short, reactors. Although these players are necessary foils for the few true actors, even they must be selected with care. A mammoth spectacle employing a "cast of thousands" is not necessarily good, any more than is a world made better by overpopulation.

The big trouble is, as Jimmy Durante used to say, "Everybody wants ta get inta de act." Satanism has done nothing to discourage the would-be fool to step on stage, it has left him at the mercy of the severest critics — his fellow creatures. He has no God smiling from the balcony and providing him with even a scant round of applause. No kindly deity will chuckle at his lousy jokes nor nod approval at his histrionics.

Thus, Satanism serves as the Great Separation Process. Consequently Satanism can be disastrous for those who see it as a short-cut to godsmanship. I have often said that the popularity of occultism and the waning of orthodox religion can be attributed to the "do-it-yourself-God kit" factor. Man feels he can control, at least in part, his own destiny, rather than the Greyhound Bus deity doing the driving for him. As such, occultists in general and Satanists in particular place themselves on stage in a manner never before seen.

Obviously one alternative to obstacles arising from such "mastery" of one's self is to grab a spear and try to support the leading players as competently as possible. Another alternative is to leave the stage completely and become part of a discerning audience. The third and only other escape from the drama is to leave the theater. What then can one do? Search for other spectacles and amusements where a measure of recognition or at least enjoyment might be found? Impossible. The World Stage never varies in its presentation. To become an actor one must be unique. To become a reactor one requires sensitivity. To become a member of the audience requires discrimination. To leave the theater means annihilation of mind and body.

Yes, the world is not simply a stage, but a Barnum and Bailey world, just as phony as it can be. For the world to become any more truthful, we'd all better come to grip with the facts. I like to think that Satanists are more likely to have the scales fall from their eyes. It helps me keep the faith.

Nonconformity
Satanism's Greatest Weapon

AN INDIVIDUALIST MUST ALWAYS LIVE IN HIS OWN WORLD, NOT ONE CREATED BY others' standards. There will always be plenty of people who will share a nonconformist's world with him and be as happy for it as the maverick might be to have others share his.

The very essence of Satanism is described by its semantic designation, *The Other.* A person who comfortably accepts the dictates of popular culture might be sympathetic or even enthused about Satanism, but he cannot be termed a Satanist. A true Satanist, even if unspoken, must be responsible for reaction and change.

It has been argued that conformity is comfortable, and so it is, if it agrees with one's digestion. Some individuals cannot eat whatever is placed before them, however. Unfortunately, a starving person will usually eat indiscriminantly, and once his belly is full, even begins to like it. Most people, being emotionally starved animals, lack imagination and personality and are content to accept whatever is imposed upon them, unless, of course, they are told they must worry or become angry over certain issues. Planned protest is no different than programmed complacency to a real Satanist.

A Satanist should not allow himself to be programmed by others. He should fight tooth and nail against it, for that is the greatest enemy to his freedom of spirit. It is the very denial of life itself, which was given to him for a wondrous, unique experience — not for imitation of the colorless existence of others.

If the definition of magic is "the change in situation or events in accordance with one's will, which would, using normally accepted methods, be unchangeable," it would seem that any successful magical working is an act of nonconformity. The greater one's natural degree of nonconformity, the greater are one's magical powers. One's will, particularly as it pertains to magical success, is an important commodity. But strong-willed should not be confused with willfulness. Just about everyone nowadays is an extremely willful zombie, blustering along on wills not their own. Grim determination abounds, but it comes second-hand. Its motivation does not emanate from the creative region of the brain, only the response centers.

A person devoid of special ability must work harder to become "special," which often results in an abrasive pretense of infallibility. Combine the overachiever's pseudo-specialty with his hauteur of infallibility, and all that's lacking to complete the profile of contemporary "cool" is freeze-dried nonconformity. If nonconformity is Satanism's strength, planned or put-on nonconformity is its greatest weakness. The predictable antics of heavy-handed "Satanists" are quite profitably exploited by non-Satanists.

I foresee a return to slavery, once money becomes worthless. In fact, it will become more desirable to become a self-realized, pleasing slave than a silly, incompetent master. The ratio of masters to slaves is today an unrecognized lampoon. Now that everyone's a big shot and everything's a big deal, it doesn't appear as if slavery exists. It does, but in a half-assed way. Only the term is taboo: out of earshot, out of mind. When there is no buying power, only barter and human desirability will be of value. Then, those who can accomplish things will be in demand, rather than those who simply exist and collect their checks.

The reversal of sacred or tiresome standards, whether they are attitudinal or sensory, is the better part of true nonconformity. That's why the reverse status of the slave is coming into its own. When it is realized that puffed-up inadequacy without buying power is a liability, you'll begin seeing the following slogan: "It is better to be used than to be useless."

Anyone's identity rests upon recognition, appreciation — in short, the knowledge that he or she has a reason for existing. We know that a multitude exist for no other reason that to keep the money circulating. What this multitude can purchase buys them their illusory identity. The multitude actually buy into the notion that they are important. Or do they? Is there a demon within each of them jabbing a pitchfork of doubt? I believe there is. That is why they're quick to air their feelings, that they believe "something is wrong," even though they can't quite identify what it is. They are smugly pleased that the jobs they goldbrick —

which could be done in a fraction of the time by fewer people — pay such a good wage. They're leisure-time activity oriented (vital for a variety of industries), yet they are nagged by the thought that "something is wrong."

That "something wrong" is despondency based upon a feeling of inadequacy, compounded by illusions of worthiness and pretensions of importance. In the future, human beings will be barter. It's time humans became accustomed to it.

How to be God
(Or The Devil)

THOSE WITH ILLUSIONS OF OMNIPOTENCE SHOULD CONSIDER THE PREREQUISITES for deification. If you really have the makings of a Higher Being, here are some handy guidelines:

1) Don't advertise. Just let your presence be known. Never, under any conditions, go around proclaiming yourself the Devil. Others must recognize you as such. The reason the God of the Christians — the fiction known as Christ — doesn't make regular appearances at concerts, book-signing parties or backyard barbeques is because he doesn't have to. There are plenty of followers who will advertise his existence for him, not to mention attesting to personal acquaintanceship. If you are a first-rate devil, others will do your advertising for you (whether you ask for it or not).

2) Never be fashionable; always be mysterious and enigmatic. Remember: man follows his gods, and his gods are never trendy. You never met a God who wanted to be one of the crowd. That's why it has been said that "The Lord works in mysterious ways." Or why an unexpected catastrophe is called "an act of God."

3) You must be creative. Take inspiration from the most sordid sources if necessary, but never imitate. Rip-off artists cannot proclaim themselves divinities because they lack the originality or creativity to come up with fresh ideas, let alone new worlds.

4) You must have style. Class. Be reserved. Show some restraint. If you can't be decorous around other people, how can you maintain order and control?

5) A sense of humor is a must; a god who can't laugh at himself or find comic relief is a dull Jehovah and most definitely un-Satanic.

6) Always harbor some doubt, even about yourself. The booby hatches are filled with megalomaniacs who are cocky sure of their own

omnipotence. A modicum of self-doubt in the god business adds up to the sort of self-awareness most mortals lack, which leads to our next decree.

7) Be aware of your own mortality. Understand that gods have been proclaimed dead many times throughout history. That's why they have Valhallas and Avalons and lands like Nod, east of Eden.

8) You must be perceptive enough to see things as they really are, not how you might have been taught by others who stand to gain from your ignorance. Yet to better understand the ways of man and deal with him, you must be able to suspend your awareness of what's really happening and see things through his eyes. In other words, learn to be stupid if it will serve you best.

9) Be merciful, especially when you're happy, but cruel if you're pissed off. If you really wield any power, people will realize the benefits gained by contributing to your happiness, or the tough luck that can befall them by getting you sore.

Fernando DePlancy
An Intimate Glimpse of a Little-Known Satanist

IT IS DOUBTFUL THAT MOST READERS OF OCCULT LITERATURE WILL COME across the name Fernando DePlancy. The man and his works are well known in the fields of microbiology and genetics; few seekers of the lore of ceremonial magic are, however, aware of the vast contributions he has made.

DePlancy was born to humble parents in Lisbon, Portugal, on September 28, 1887. His mother, Felicia, and father, Humberto, were getting on in years when little Fernando, the last of eight children, was born. If we are to believe historians, Fernando's parents felt ill-equipped to raise their child, and migrated to the Azores after finding a maiden aunt to care for him. Soon growing to young manhood, Fernando and aunt moved to England and took up residence a short distance from Blackpool with a couple who operated a small roadside pub. Unbeknownst to Fernando, MacGregor Mathers — who was to become Aleister Crowley's mentor — was a frequent visitor to the tavern. It seems likely that Mathers initiated the lad into the mysteries of the Golden Dawn. No one knows exactly how much magical curricula Fernando underwent.

In 1905, at the age of 18, Fernando emigrated to America. Unable to afford college, he took a position in Buffalo, N.Y. as a baggage boy at the train depot. Meanwhile he devoured all books on scientific themes that he could lay his hands on. One such volume was Captain John G. Bourke's *Scatologic Rites of All Nations*. Chapter 24, "Obscene Survivals in the Games of English Rustics," especially intrigued him, as did the chapter containing extracts from the writings of Dioscorides and the views of Galen in connection with the medicinal use of cerumen, or ear wax. He read Rosinus Lentilius' *Physico-Medicarum,* which relates that "there was a certain old hypochondriac, of fifty or more, who, in order to ease himself of an obstinate constipation, for more than a month drank copious draughts of his own urine, fresh and hot, but with the worst results."

Young DePlancy felt his destiny promised more than baggage handling. Leaving his job at the railway station, he devoted all of his time to his studies, which by that time had developed to the level of experimentation. Drawing again from Lentilius, DePlancy discovered Christian Franz Paullini's *Filth Pharmacy* (published in Frankfurt, 1696). The only available English translation (by Smith and Pratz) left much to be desired and could not be relied upon. Several bouts with insomnia inspired DePlancy to ingest donkey dung as per Paullini's directions. Though he found his sleep improved, his dreams got worse. Nightmares were preferable to sleeplessness, and so DePlancy extracted from the same sourcebook a remedy for vertigo which had been disturbing him since he fell from a hayloft as a child. DePlancy's discovery of the medicinal value of peacock droppings deserves more than a cursory glance; it suggests a long dormant association of this bird with both Satanism and moon worship. The peacock, we know, was the bird that drew the car of Juno, and that goddess was as much a lunar deity as Diana.

Taking one-gram doses of the droppings improved DePlancy's condition to such an extent that he could climb to the roof of his lodging and stand at its edge without the slightest dizziness. It was during one of his nocturnal rooftop vigils that Fernando espied the lighted window of a neighboring building, which had the reputation of being a house of ill-repute. With no shades drawn, it was apparent that the lighted room was the washroom. Soon a man appeared before the squalid toilet basin and relieved himself. Moments after he left, a rather dowdy woman entered to answer the call of nature.

DePlancy began to reel. Not from any sordid sexual motivation, but in recollection of what he had read on page 337 of Bourke's aforementioned book on scatologic rites. It was a personal letter from Professor E. N. Horsford of Harvard University to Captain Bourke stating, "I have been recently informed, by a man who is acquainted with the peculiarities of Parisian Life, that there are men who are in the habit of swallowing the scum which they obtain from street urinals, and they are known as 'Les mangeurs du blanc.'" It was at that moment of heightened epiphany that Fernando DePlancy grasped what his life's work was to be.

Sometime in the spring of 1910, DePlancy, feeling that in order to expand his knowledge and develop his theories he must venture further afield than Buffalo, New York, set out to tour the back roads and byways of America. He had saved a modest research fund from his earnings at the whorehouse, where he had persuaded the lady in charge to engage him as a part-time janitor and stiff towel collector. Though his remuneration was small, DePlancy was more than rewarded by certain activities that were germane to his studies. I will not bore the reader with unimportant details of his departure and first stages of his travels, other than to mention that while in Peoria he was robbed of his wallet by a pickpocket who deftly reached into his lowered trousers while he sat in the cubicle of a public toilet. The "crapper-worker" was apprehended the following week in the same lavatory, but having spent DePlancy's money was unable to make restitution. That justice had been served and the culprit sent to jail was of little help to Fernando's pocketbook. Fortunately he had pinned a reserve supply of cash to his undershirt, and with that sum was able to proceed on his journey.

A big breakthrough came in Arkansas, where DePlancy met the famous author and chronicler of latrinalia, Chic Sales. Together DePlancy and Sales explored their interests as far West as Waco, whence DePlancy proceeded alone to El Paso. It was in this city that Fernando discovered the delights of the beer from the country south of the border. Known as *cerveza,* it was substantially different from the English ale to which DePlancy had become accustomed in his youth. Interestingly, the Latin name for beer or ale is *cerevisia,* which would seem to be a derivative from the name of that goddess employed in her libations, and held sacred as the means of producing the condition of inebriation, which in pagan nations had been looked upon as sacred. Exploring this custom of antiquity, DePlancy remained in El Paso for the better part of 28 years in relative obscurity, consuming large quantities of *cerveza.*

In 1938, a government official in charge of recreating an authentic American slum for the Federal Building exhibit at the forthcoming World's Fair in San Francisco espied DePlancy in a drunken state sleeping under the urinal in the men's room of a local cantina. Prodding him gently with his foot, he awakened Fernando, who wakened and explained that he had fallen asleep from the fatigue of his research. Within 24 hours, both scholar and sponsor were headed for California on a Santa Fe Pullman car. It was contracted that throughout the duration of the fair DePlancy would recline in a littered doorway of the proposed slum complex. Adjacent to the tableau was to be a theatre, where every two hours a film, *One Third of a Nation*, would be shown to visitors touring the mock slum. While the film presentation was in progress, DePlancy would be free to "take a break," as it were. As it developed, Fernando discovered means to peep into the restrooms of the attraction, and did so whenever time and circumstances permitted, thus furthering his research.

The reader may now be wondering what bearing Fernando's studies and lifestyle had to do with his subsequent contribution to Satanism.

In 1943, at the age of 56, Fernando DePlancy was working as a tool checker at an aircraft plant in Burbank, California, helping his Uncle Sam (he had since become a U.S. citizen) with the war effort. One morning a bright and cheerful young lady approached him with a request for a monkey wrench. Something about her face seemed familiar. As it turned out, she had sat next to DePlancy on a bus the previous day. They exchanged pleasantries and in the course of conversation she revealed that it was her great-uncle who was young Fernando's guardian at the roadside pub in England. The young lady's current husband was a flyer with the R. A. F. and the third cousin twice removed of Aleister Crowley. The two became fast friends, during which time Beryl (which was the young lady's name) initiated DePlancy into the mysteries of the Grampian Flagellants while the older DePlancy imparted essentials of his years of research to his new friend. A ritualistic alliance had indeed been established, and soon the two, in concert, were paving the way for the stuff of which latter-day journalists would be able to relate to an emerging Church of Satan. Unfortunately, Beryl returned to England only to discover that her marriage was invalid and she had been deceived. She later married a pathetic young man and was subsequently murdered by John Christie of the infamous 10 Rillington Place. Fernando DePlancy, having become a full-blown admitted devil-worshipper, was killed on August 14, 1945, when he was struck by a flying toilet which had been ripped loose by a victory celebrant and thrown from the balcony of the theater in which he sat watching *God is My Co-Pilot*.

Erotic Crystallization Inertia

THAT WHICH IS PLEASING TO THE EYE GIVES JOY, AND JOY GIVES STRENGTH, and strength gives life. We receive pleasure in many ways and by diverse means, but the most conscious of all is through eye-appeal. Man is a visually-oriented animal. He establishes standards of visual attractiveness of an inflexible nature. If the standards he has set forth for beauty are modified by fashion or social change, he will never be quite as happy as before the change took place. As he grows older and styles change more, he will cling to the substance of his joy by retreating into social circles where he might reminisce of what once made him happy. In this way he maintains his vitality, albeit vicariously. With his cronies he will talk of the "good old days" — days replete with the sights so dear to him, now so sadly changed. His pals and the elderly girls who abound in the old compound share his nostalgia, and their clothing is out of style. Out of style! How fortunate for the inmates of senior citizens' centers that they can maintain at least some semblance of the "good old days," if only on their backs. Little do they realize that this very out-datedness is keeping them alive.

How often it is seen that when an aging person loses interest in life, when his children have grown up and his vitality decreases, he will enter a retirement community and suddenly become revitalized. Theoretically, it would be assumed that such an atmosphere would hasten the death process, add to the inertia of old age. Why does the opposite invariably occur? Because the aging person is suddenly thrown into a controlled environment, one where there is more visual imagery conducive to his excitement and enthusiasm than the outside world. Stylishly out of style, it becomes fun for the codgers to look at each other, much as it must have been fun in their younger days, the boys gazing with lust at the girls, and the girls longing for the boys.

And what about the small towns, those places bypassed by the freeways where octogenarians dominate the landscape, the little jerkwater towns where nobody ever seems to die, where they all seem so crotchety over what is going on in the world, fighting over any change that will alter the visual landscape, and only accepting that which promises freedom from pain, illness and death. From a visual point of view, these places are completely inert: cars are 20 years old, no buildings are ever torn down. Much time is spent on porches and park benches, around pot-bellied stoves, at the bus depot, wherever there is something to be seen! And what is seen? The same things that have always been seen.

The inhabitants of such a place might not live to be 100 years old (although there exist such environments in which numbers of incredibly old people abound). It appears certain, however, that in static environments there are more old people per capita than within a constantly-changing scene. It will be argued that it is natural for old people to live in such places while it is stifling to young persons. This is true, but it need not be. The main reason young people leave such environments is because they can't cope with the old farts. The old folks feel equally disdainful of the "progress" that is manifested in youthful styles — fully as alien to their visual joy associations as their stodginess is to the young.

Under such conflicting standards of visual exhilaration, no one can be nearly so happy as if a totally compatible visual atmosphere were to prevail. Let us not forget that the young of today are crystallizing their own visual standards of beauty. Soon enough they will become the old fogeys. In time they will band together in retirement communities and old people's homes, reminiscing and surrounding themselves with accoutrements of their youth.

Places where people live longest are space-time warps. They could live even longer if young people dressed and looked exactly like themselves. The chronological change that accompanies style change is the culprit here. With each new advance in medical science, there is a setback another way insofar as longevity is concerned. While men of science discover cures, they also discover means of communication and travel that open wide the very isolation that harbors uniquely collective existences. Thus Shangri-Las are turned into Manhattans and germ-laden, dying 90-year-olds are turned into germ-free, smog-smothered, anxiety-ridden dying 60-year-olds.

Just as fashion centers of the world promote the quick death, so unchanging environments exist as hubs of longevity. The most deadly lie is the half-truth, and the fashion industry has perpetuated one of the most eloquent of all, namely that a fresh, new approach is what keeps one young. The fresh approach does keep one young, if the person is fresh, young and vital in spirit.

The freshest thing that an old man can see is a pretty girl dressed in a manner that is reminiscent of his youthful erotic crystallization. Erotically stimulating but also emotionally acceptable. Likewise, an elderly lady will zestfully witness a handsome young man ("fresh young blood") attired in the manner of the suitors she once attracted. She can (and does) vicariously maintain an aura of attractiveness when confronted by such a man, and it is this very aura, constantly recharged, that will sustain her very life.

When the world one loves is seen to be dying, the viewer dies a little with it. A great American painter, Reginald Marsh, exemplifies this truism. Every day until his death at the age of 56, he sketched and painted the most earthy, sweaty and lusty examples of humanity he could lay his eyes upon. His productive voyeurism led him through the entire spectrum of cheap cafes, carnivals, amusement parks, skid rows, exclusive clubs, opera openings, coming-out parties and everything in-between. His super-realistic canvases were jammed with the kind of people he loved to watch in the environments he loved to haunt.

As his closing years approached, Reginald Marsh grew depressed at the changing scene. New styles were emerging and it now became more difficult to immerse himself in the vistas from which he had so long drawn, both in his paintings and life itself. His canvases of lumpy women and pot-bellied men were too unappealing for the "think thin" era of the 1950s, and his floozies violated the then-current Grace Kelly/Ivory Soap look. His disdain for modern masters ("Matisse draws like a three-year-old, "Picasso ... a false front") became exemplified as he summed up modern art as "high and pure and sterile — no sex, no drink, no muscles."

Marsh's "out of date" feeling reached its zenith when he was asked to take part in an art symposium. The first speaker, who was a then-popular New York painter, enthusiastically championed current trends. Then followed a professor who advocated new and dynamic experimentation in visual appeal. At last it was Reginald Marsh's turn to speak. He stood on the platform for a moment, as if trying to collect his thoughts. A sad look of resignation appeared in his eyes as he gazed down at the audience. The talented watcher of his innermost secret lusts and life-giving scintillations declared softly, "I am not a man of this century," and sat down. He died shortly thereafter.

Anyone who is satisfied with the way things are going is reluctant to change his mode of living. This includes style, fashion and environment. Man is the only animal who has been carefully taught to be discontent. What is even worse, man is the only animal who has been educated on one hand to be discontented while religion has programmed him to remain static, inert and complacent. Small wonder he is such a mass of frustrations.

If he is content with the way things are going, the priests of fashion and change coerce him into unwilling and unnecessary modification. If he is a malcontent who wishes to escape from the world he feels is short-changing him, he is told to accept things as they are, be thankful for small favors and await his better life in a future paradise.

Evocation

THE AVERAGE PERSON HAS ONE MAJOR FLAW THAT PEGS HIM AS A PERENNIAL adolescent once he leaves his childhood. And that is the inability to participate in or to experience anything resembling a personality that diverges from his immutable emotional crystallization at the time of his adolescence. This crystallization is carried with him as an unyielding, tightly strapped knapsack which contains all of the limited elements relative to his narrow field of emotional response.

The more limited one's "bag" the easier it is to see what's inside. The lesser man readily advertises the contents of his bag, leaving himself open to manipulation on the part of the wizard. The wizard, having ascertained the substance of his quarry's limited emotional stimuli, needs simply to drive his attack home without concern for the possibility of his quarry defending himself. The magician, on the other hand, is able to respond to diverse situations with balanced emotional involvement. If a magician is attacked through his emotional attachment to one situation, he can escape the attack by involving himself in another equally compelling situation. The lesser man never realizes this, and consequently becomes befuddled when, after first "doing his dance" and temporarily winning the higher man over, moves in for the kill only to find that the higher man is no longer running with him and is nowhere to be seen. Children have not yet packed their "bag." They enjoy the delights of many settings and situations irrespective of any connection they might have with one another. A child is not bound by the bureaucracy of the mind that ensnares the lesser elder person. Each child is a minute renaissance man.

It is one thing to be narrow-minded out of choice, but quite a different thing to be narrow-minded when one has never known how to be broad-minded. If a person has been open-minded in the early stage of adulthood there is a good chance to become selectively narrow-minded later in life. Bigotry is exhilarating if taken up with careful deliberation and is only self-destructive when ingrained as part of the personality. It is the difference between indulgence and compulsion. Indulgence can be controlled; compulsion controls. One of the greatest magical devices therefore is to become open to gratifying emotional stimuli like a child, but close-minded when the whole will must be employed.

The lesser man equates everything in his life by the standards of emotion that happen to be strapped inside his "bag," his constipated realm of being. If horses are his thing, he has little use for auto races. He is moved by Bach and Baroque splendor but cannot relate emotionally to Country and Western music. The sight of a pith helmet and the words of Kipling evokes no vision or sense of a barracks near the Khyber.

How many situations move you to emotional response which borders on total identification with the given situation? Test yourself to see how totally you can become a sounding board for random situations; be as one, so to speak, with the total emotional response from a situation which needs but a subtle cue to get into motion. This is what children and wizards find easy.

Before anyone can expect to progress in magical prowess, he must expand his consciousness but not at the expense of his emotions! Drugs expand the consciousness quickly and effortlessly but make only one major emotional response possible, and that is for the God directly responsible for the changeover, the drug itself.

There is only one fly in this great potential sea of ointment. If one does not already respond to the varying stimuli of life around him, then no amount of exercise will make it possible. Pathetic, isn't it? No magical future. No fortune. No hope. Oh, how man will keep trying. Reading grimoires, taking metaphysical study courses, self-help programming, pills, philtres, smokes or whatever will enable him to love that which he does not already! One cannot teach receptivity to sensation, but one can create a conducive environment in which one might prepare himself for the art of evocation.

The essence of any magical working is a *complete* evocation. It Is more important to experience total emotional response to one's environment than all the "occult" knowledge in the world. How pitifully few are capable of a strong evocation! The most wonderful thing of all is the ability to enter another dimension — another realm of being — and feel the wholeness of that other realm to the exclusion of all other environments.

Music is the most effective tool for evocation, as the entire body rhythm is helplessly taken up by the pattern of life associated with the musical selection. A meaningful idea never dies, nor does the emotional response generated by certain compositions. If enough people are inspired or moved by these compositions, the selections become sonic repository for the accumulated emotions of all those affected by them. Becoming an all-encompassing sensing element to the collective feedback of a particular composition can yield a total evocation.

With certain exceptions, the best place to produce such an evocation is a hard-walled, vast enclosure that will trap the music, just opposite to the way that a pentagon of mirrors will send forth imagery. A "live" enclosure producing echo and reverberation will reflect the substance of the music, forming a "sound trap." A sound trap has much the same effect as a light trap — both are devices employed for the internalization of thought matter, whereby the ecstatic evocation will ensue. All actions and feelings, situations and environments associated with the music involved contributes to the wondrous synthesis that becomes your evocation. The acoustics of the bullring, the circus tent, the ice-skating rink, the vaulted cathedral render all excellent sound-traps. The sound-retention of a ballroom, auditorium, theatre, etc., is such that combined with the emotional stimulus present (a partner dancing closely in one's arms, a tragic play, an heroic spectacle, etc.), the nearest approximation to a strong evocation that most humans might approach will be achieved.

Evocation through musical internalization demands concentration. The more people present the less chance the magician has to properly experience the music, with the possible exception of the concert hall, which is built for this express purpose. The more extraneous factors, the greater the magician is distracted from his evocation. Though enjoyment might be heightened by listening to music with kindred souls, it is easier to achieve ecstasy when one is not concerned with what others might think.

Profound emotional response to music does not necessarily make an evocation, but an evocation is always a profound emotional experience. An evocation is an entire state of being, triggered by a "key" (music in this case), which in itself is but a distillation or capsule of the total evocation subsequently attained.

Music For the Ritual Chamber

MUSIC THAT ACCOMPANIES YOUR RITUAL MUST INTENSIFY THE EMOTIONS
necessary for the particular working. Music is a language in itself, and,
like all other languages, if used indiscriminately, becomes both insincere
and meaningless. The most popular selections soon burn themselves
out through overexposure, and only when they have gone unplayed for
a period of time can they assume classic status.

A pleasing musical selection can easily become a habit, in fact, a
compulsion. Eventually, through constant play, it will lose its appeal.
Any habit can be broken by overexposure. Therefore, when selecting
music for the ritual chamber, you must be able to hear and react to it in
a fresh and enthusiastic manner. For this reason I recommend that any
selections you find emotionally exciting enough to evoke a decided
reaction must be put aside and preserved for ritualistic purposes.

Without a doubt the most effective selections are not those which
foster introspection, but those which convey an image. This, essentially,
is the difference between "mystical" and "magical" music. "Mystical"
music is retentive in nature and does not impinge itself upon your consciousness. "Magical" music attacks your senses and impels a decided
emotional response. Any music which can be listened to without your
being consciously aware of its presence can be considered mystical in
nature, even though its tempo may be fast and its volume loud.

Music commonly heard piped into public areas is generally programmed so as to exert an influence on the hearer even though he is
not listening. This type of music is utilized for lesser magical purposes
(maintaining production flow, inducing eating and drinking, stimulating
shoppers to buy, etc.). The music's provider employs it towards magical
ends; those who hear it are controlled by it, rather than using it to control.

If you are unmoved by music, it is not always due to a lack of emotion. Perhaps you cannot separate and isolate varying frequencies of

sound — in short, you may be tone deaf. An emotional response to various musical tones occurs when a unique combination of space, time, and sound converges into a single unit. Each living creature with properly functioning sound receptors (including animals, birds, fish, and even plants) has within its being a "tuned" set of "strings." Just how each is tuned depends upon many contributing factors, both hereditary and environmental.

Let us say, in order to simplify matters, that there is a separate chord tuned for each emotional response. In "lower" animals and plants, there is less of a diversity of chords — only pleasure and pain. Pleasure makes a cat purr, and pain makes it fight. Humans have added certain chords to their internal lyre, such as sentiment, which sometimes appears as nostalgia — a combination of pleasure and pain. Humans' internal chording is more complex because humans experience a wider range of stimuli than do other animals (though, alas, the reverse is often true).

Certain intervals of sound are almost universal in their emotional effect. And they can be formulated. Hence, there are compositions which are relatively made to order for ceremonial use. Though there is some divergence of response between Eastern and Western ears, certain combinations of sound engenders atavistic responses analogous to all human beings.

Which musical selections would I choose for ceremonial purposes? First of all, I would combine passages from several compositions, even though it may involve editing. I often solve this time-consuming problem by accompanying the rite on the organ. I have recorded myself playing in order that I may experience the additional satisfaction of partially creating the music which is required. The organ is put on "automatic pilot", and pre-recorded music issues forth or an assistant takes over.

For a Gothic mood which will enhance an archetypical Satanic Mass, the organ works of Bach, Couperin, Vidor, Franck, and Palestrina are perfect. Faure's *Requiem* and *Pavanne* likewise.

For a less-traditional yet strong element of solemnity, try the second movement from Beethoven's Seventh Symphony, the second movement from Tchaikovsky's Fourth Symphony, or Berlioz' *Funeral and Triumphal Symphony*. If you wish to invoke feelings of power, nothing can beat the following: the opening measures of Gomez' Overture to *Il*

Guarany, the crashing climax to the first act of Puccini's *Turandot,* Wagner's overture to *Tannhaüser,* and his Magic Fire Music and Ride of the Valkyries from *Die Walkure,* the finale of Lalo's *Le Roi d'ys,* the Napoleon Bevonulasa from Kodaly's *Hary Janos,* The Great Gate at Kiev from Mussorgsky's *Pictures at an Exhibition,* and *Also Sprach Zarathustra* by Richard Strauss.

A transition between power, compassion and sacred love can be effected by compositions like Handel's Largo from *Xerxes,* the Trio and Apotheosis from Gounod's *Faust,* Va Pensiero from Verdi's *Nabucco,* the Overture to von Flotow's *Martha,* Sibelius' *Finlandia,* the "Dracula" theme from Tchaikovsky's *Swan Lake,* the same composer's overture to *Romeo and Juliet,* Wagner's Liebestod from *Tristan and Isolde,* and the Granadinas from Callejo-Barrera's *Emigrantes.*

For purely sensual purposes, the unholy musical trinity surely must be Ravel's *Bolero,* Orff's *Carmina Burana* and the Bacchanale from Saint-Saens' *Samson and Delilah.*

These are but a few of the seemingly endless lists of suitable musical selections, chosen at random and based upon productive past use. I have excluded evocative music of a more popular nature because, like everyone else, I have my personal favorites which are readily identifiable with meaningful situations. Perhaps one day I shall share them with you, and it will be seen that many Satanists — like other emotionally responsive individuals — favor the same tunes!

Hymn of the Satanic Empire

or

Battle Hymn of the Apocalypse

Words and music
by Anton LaVey

Transcription-
Reuben Radding

(No chords)

1)Drums out of the dark-ness lis-ten well   Drums beat-ing like thun-der
2)Once there was a need for sim-ple minds.   Once there was a need to

straight from hell   Trum-pets are blar-ing,   the time's come 'round
save men's souls.   Fools had to be forced to   stay in line

Sa- tan is here to   claim his ground,   there's an
preach- ers and bi- bles   could serve those goals,   with their

Dmin   G   C   E7 Amin   F   D7/F#

Earth that's green, there's   an Earth that's free, there's   a place for you and   a
ho- ly writ and   their card' nal sin they   could force their pap-er

G   A   Dmin   G   C   E7 Amin

place for me. But the   bleed- ing hearts would- n't let   it be, we   don't
de- mons in to a   card- board pri- son,   a pa- per cell, they   can't

F   G   C   A   Dmin   G   C   E7Amin

need them a - ny more.   Let the lions and ti-gers   rip them up The A-
do that a - ny

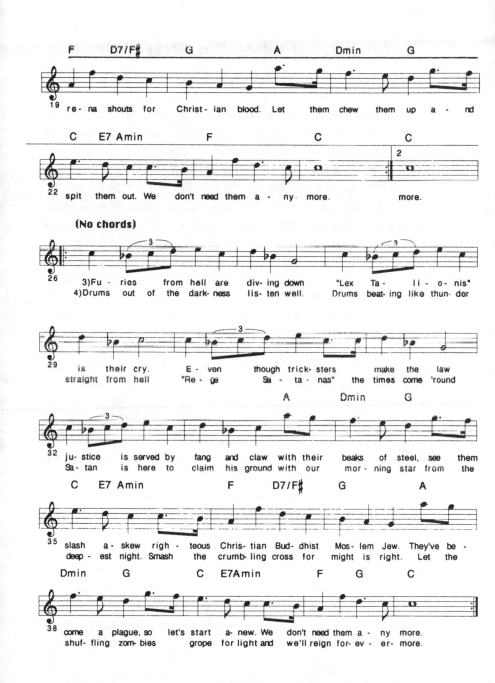

Evangelists Vs. The New God

IT COMES AS NO SURPRISE THAT THE TELEVANGELISTS ARE BEING CASHIERED ON all fronts, either through scandal or absurdity. People are wising up about the Swaggerts and the Roberts and Bakkers only because it is time for them to be allowed to wise up. Why? Because the Christ-sellers were beginning to compete with the very god that they were employing: TV.

In previous centuries, the Church was the great controller, dictating morality, stifling free expression and posing as conservator of all great art and music. Today we have television dictating fashions, thoughts, attitudes, objectives as once did the Church, using many of the same techniques but doing it so palatably that no one notices. Instead of "sins" to keep people in line, we have fear of being judged unacceptable by our peers (by not wearing the right running shoes, not drinking the right kind of beer or wearing the wrong kind of deodorant), and fear of imposed insecurity concerning our own identities. Borrowing the Christian sole salvation concept, television tells people that only through exposure to TV can the sins of alienation and ostracism be absolved.

We don't have to go out early Sunday mornings to get religion — that was too much work. Now all we have to do is click the remote control and church comes to us. We're intimate with television's comforting presence from the moment we pop out of our mother's womb; indeed, TV is omnipresent, shadowing us more than the obsolete God shadowed Joan of Arc. There are television sets in every home, every restaurant, every hotel room, every shopping mall — now they're even small enough to carry in your pocket like electronic rosaries. It is an unquestioned part of everyday life. Kneeling before the cathode ray God, with our *TV Guide* concordance in hand, we maintain the illusion of choice by flipping channels (chapters and verses). It doesn't matter what is flashing on the screen — all that's important is that the TV stays on.

When the Church based its mandate on the Holy Bible as the word of God Almighty, it brought out the doubters because their claim betrayed a glaring lack of logic. The Holy Fathers devised the necessity for "faith" in hopes of covering up the inherent problems. But when TV masquerades as "entertainment," there's no room for doubt. No absurd premises are being advanced, so no one has any cause to resist. No matter how much a free thinker you believe you are, there is still the influence of television in your life. To deny TV now would be as atheistic as Ingersoll denying the existence of God.

Naturally the televangelists had to be cut off — they were alienating the sheep from the shepherd. The ends are the same as they always have been. Sheep must be kept in line and encouraged to deposit money in the right places. But the televangelists became too greedy in their invoking of God, siphoning off too big a chunk of money for themselves.

That's why the present "religious war" isn't between any forces of "Good" and "Evil." It is being waged between Media (the State) vs. Churches (Catholic and otherwise) who are tying up millions of dollars of valuable property and assets. As Satanists, we have the advantage of realizing this early in the game. It has never been enough for us to be atheistic — we have learned how to smash religious ignorance by beating them at their own game, using the Christians' own manufactured fears to destroy them.

We can use TV as a potent propaganda machine. The stage is set for the infusion of true Satanic philosophy and potent (emotionally inspiring) music to accompany the inverted crosses and pentagrams. Instead of holding our rituals in chambers designed for a few dozen people, we are moving into auditoriums crowded with ecstatic Satanists thrusting their fists forward in the sign of the horns. As much "bad press" as the Church of Satan has received from the media over the past few years — Satanic child abuse, sacrifices, etc. — mention of *The Satanic Bible* only points people in our direction. Perhaps that's the plan, after all.

The key is to use television and not be used by it. Munitions makers don't try the new stuff out on themselves. If it takes turning your television to the wall or throwing it out the window, do it. We are adversaries to be reckoned with, and must not be taken in by our own infernal devices. We must allow stratification to develop so that a world for the vital and living can be established and maintained.

Some Evidence of a New Satanic Age Part 2

IN *THE SATANIC BIBLE* I PROVIDED SOME EXAMPLE OF HOW MODERN Christianity was modifying itself to keep in step with diabolical advances. Now it's time to recognize yet another manifestation. Many of you have already read my writings identifying TV as the new God. There is a little thing I neglected to mention up until now — television is the major mainstream infiltration of the New Satanic religion.

The birth of TV was a magical event foreshadowing its Satanic significance. The first commercial broadcast was aired on Walpurgisnacht, April 30th, 1939, at the New York World's Fair. Since then, TV's infiltration has been so gradual, so complete, that no one even noticed. People don't need to go to church any more; they get their morality plays on television. What began modestly as rabbit ears on top of family TV sets are now satellite sishes and antennas pridefully dominating the skyline, replacing crosses on top of churches. The TV set, or Satanic family altar, has grown more elaborate since the early 50s, from the tiny, fuzzy screen to huge "entertainment centers" covering entire walls with several TV monitors. What started as an innocent respite from everyday life has become in itself a replacement for real life for millions, a major religion of the masses.

The consumer society in which we now live is an extension of the society once governed by religion for many centuries. Instead of obeying the holy bible, right or wrong, TV advertising now instructs what to buy and what not to buy. Atheism wasn't tolerated when scriptural dictates were in fashion and accepted as the Word. Now, thanks to Satanic infiltration, it's safe to say, "I don't believe in God." But modern heresy — not conforming to a television lifestyle, not accepting television truths — is liable to be punished with as much righteous enthusiasm as ever.

The clergy of the TV religion are those entertainers, newscasters in particular, who nightly spread the Word from their cathode-ray pulpit. The network newscasters are the High Priests and High Priestesses of Satanism, bending the minds of viewers to the requirements of consumer marketing. The local newscasters are the parish priests, yawking, ribbing and emoting over the latest local tragedies. Celebrities, whether local or national, are all part of the hierarchy of the church, men of the cloth. There should be no complaint regarding network High Priests arriving to report on scenes of devastation in white stretch limos. After all, they are royalty within the Church and should be accorded the same privileges as a visiting Pope, Cardinal or Archbishop.

There is no way a person can escape religion as long as he is living in a religious environment. Situation comedies, dramatic series and soap operas are broadcast day and night seven days a week to activate and sustain the lifestyles of the parishioners, where before only fanatics practiced daily devotions. The masses committed only one day, Sunday, to the Christian God. As I've said before, the *TV Guide* is the new concordance. Tabloids and news magazines supply the instructions for pious living. TV devotion has become so pervasive that even motion pictures are today presented in the same fast-cut, limited information style.

As the Satanic stratification increases (aided by the diabolical machine), one of our tasks is to develop a graduated system to type people according to their TV lifestyle. Various levels, from spectators to stimulators, can be identified by the level of TV saturation and influence. At the bottom is the Compleat Spectator — the vegetable. At the top is the Compleat Entertainer — the ultimate provider of stimulation. Contrary to prevailing Christian values, a person who does something to hone and perfect a skill should be regarded as the most highly evolved. Someone that spends his free time doing things should receive respect and support in proportion to how productive his activity is, how solitary it is, how benign as opposed to how disruptive it is.

The TV Junkie lives his life for television. Like a religious nut, he follows everything that is going on in the media and doesn't find it necessary to know anything else. Many TV Junkies are not satisfied with keeping their knowledge to themselves and force their slave's acumen on others. They are comparable to the zealots who carry the Good Book around with them, preaching the Word of the Lord to each and every person they encounter.

The well-known Couch Potato inhabits the next level. He's an inveterate TV watcher, one who has the TV going all the time like talking wallpaper. Perhaps he has TV screens within screens, or two or three sets blasting at once. He is equivalent to the bible reader who has the Good Book present at all times, in every room — ornate family bibles in the living room, one on his nightstand, one handy in the kitchen, another reachable by the toilet. Though not quite as evangelical as the TV Junkie, the Couch Potato rarely strays out of TV range.

Next on the list is the casual Christian who watches on a fairly regular basis. Although Christian, he is nevertheless influenced by television and cannot or will not entertain anything outside the parameters of media input. The small-time parishes, inhabited by local newscasters, are the "true believers."

Finally, we get the professionals who sit atop this spectrum of religiosity, and because of the nature of their jobs, realize what must be done to maintain their professional or occupational status. Like highly-placed Vatican leaders, they never really believe what they're saying.

Once it's been resolved in a Satanist's mind that TV is a very workable proponent of Satanism in its most practical form, then he may want to remove himself from the firing line, much like the Jesuit priest or Rabbi or minister who doesn't, in his secret life, go along with every rule that he admonishes his parishioners to adhere to.

The lower clergy can deny the truth about the devilish plot behind television, but identification has been made. It will be impossible to dispel the equivalents that I've pointed out. They'll have a hitch in their brain every time they report more Satanic hysteria, knowing we consider them Priests of Satanism. It cannot help but influence their attitude, actions and behavior toward us in the future.

Sweet Slavery

SAINTHOOD, MARTYRDOM — WHAT A WASTE OF PRECIOUS MASOCHISM THAT could instead be directed towards the most profane infatuation. Love cannot exist without a master/slave relationship. But who, having known each role, would not find slavery the more desirable — nay, the only role which can be felt.

In love, even the master is constantly monitored by the contrivances necessary to sustain slavish adoration. Far better to experience total anguish. It requires no effort, demands no criteria, imposes no limits.

To be loved, feelings must be rationed. To love, the doors of hysteria, fantasy, madness may be flung open.

Pick an idol, grovel well and suffer in ecstasy. Then you in turn will be idolized four-fold by others. Just make sure your love object is not too rationally chosen, for compulsion and rationality seldom coexist. It is easier to love a tyrant, a nitwit, an anomaly, than perfection, for the masochism of love demands debasement unobtainable through sterling sources.

The pure are admired, but never desired for anything other than as soap for the soul. It is the imperfect that compels and makes a fool of one, and in foolishness is return to childhood.

A little adolescence is worth a ton of hoary profundity. That is why young love, being the most irrational, is the most consuming.

As one grows older, one does not love stronger, only more collectively. In essence, it is no longer, "Recognize me, my love," but "Remember me, my loves." Vision turned to reverie unfortunately suffers in the translation. There may be no fool like an old fool, but being a young fool is more fun, for the foolishness is fresh and invigorating, no matter how fraught with desperation.

Confessions of a Closet Misogynist

I HAVE LONG HELD W. SOMERSET MAUGHAM IN HIGH ESTEEM. HE WAS certainly a first-rate Satanist, and whatever his own sexual preoccupations may have been, he really knew women. Because of — rather than in spite of — his casting of weak, wanton, yielding and fallen women in his stories, those very females became stronger than his male characters. Like Milton's heroic Satan stealing the show from the Heavenly hosts in *Paradise Lost,* Maugham's debauched floozies emerged with stronger personas than his conscience-stricken, meaning-of-life seeking heroes. Somehow, in reducing women to weak and vulnerable creatures, humiliated as only a confirmed misogynist could portray them, Maugham evoked an essential as well as eternal female. It is that very essentialness that makes a well-adjusted, heterosexual misogynist a bulwark against the most devastating form of defeminization.

A misogynist requires an imperfect and flawed yet feminine form of woman in order to properly exercise his disdain. His disdain is, of course, based on jealousy. An overtly mannish or dominant woman creates no dualistic yearnings and is simply contemptible as a useless critter too proud for burden and not attractive enough for exploitation. In other words, it's far better to be used than to be useless. I have — since pubescent excesses and youthful errors — been a womanizer. I was never the type that girls felt secure bringing home to meet their folks. I always met my dates at prearranged and clandestine places. The fact that I appeared as a "heavy" undoubtedly elicited a certain appeal to Sweet Gwendolyn types. It was therefore understandable that aggressively passive women (yes, there is such a creature) gravitated to me. Eventually I realized that I was, because of my enthusiasm and naivete, becoming a slave to demandingly masochistic women. If that sounds like a contradiction in terms, it is. It is also a very real phenomenon, which can be depleting if unrecognized and unchecked.

There is a great deal of misunderstanding about misogyny similar to that of the stock misunderstanding of sadism. As related in *The Satanic Bible,* an epicurean sadist does not go about insulting people, pulling wings off butterflies, or tossing banana peels in front of senior citizens. An obnoxious person is invariably a latent masochist with little self-awareness that his baiting demeanor is simply punch-in-the-nose insurance. Similarly, an apparent superstud insulter of women who sprinkles his vocabulary with offensive terms for female genitalia is usually a forlorn homosexual who harbors no love/hate feelings for women. He is only aggravated by them because they are in competition for his strongest cravings: other men. He may not even admit these yearnings to himself, so he gravitates to correspondingly man-hating women, usually latent lesbians, and they clinically swing together amidst groups of other "liberated" souls.

A true misogynist is a straight man who — because he is a potential pushover for women and realizes it — resents the power a truly feminine woman wields, secretly admires this power, and seeks to capture it before it captures him. By reducing a woman to a role of servitude, he finds himself in the role of a tyrant. He wants to be a benign and considerate tyrant, but all too often a little consideration goes a short way. He really loves women but the poor things won't let him effect an expansive and pleasing sexual delineation essential to his masculinity. He consequently hates them for it. By not displaying archetypical signals of femininity they rob him of the ultimate expression of his masculinity.

It will be argued that the foregoing only indicates insecurity of one's masculine prowess or self-doubt. This is not the case, for prowess as a man is not at stake, but rather identity and counter-identity of a harmonious nature are threatened. The desired merger is one of a Yin-Yang correspondence.

It might be fair to state that a misogynist is often really punishing the "pure" female for the sins of the "impure" pretender — for whom he would either feel patronizing ridicule or else inflexible anger. Speaking for myself, I idealize Maugham's type of woman, just as the types depicted by Rubens, Renoir and Reginald Marsh. They are considered "common" types, but are actually quite uncommon. A soft, yielding, voluptuous woman with a personality to match is a rarity nowadays.

With an overabundance of the opposite kind, Pan would be hard-pressed for nymphs and could not be blamed if his syrinx went flat.

Pentagonal Revisionism
A Five-Point Program

IN RECENT YEARS WE'VE WASTED FAR TOO MUCH TIME EXPLAINING THAT SATANISM has nothing to do with kidnapping, drug abuse, child molestation, animal or child sacrifice, or any number of other acts that idiots, hysterics or opportunists would like to credit us with. Satanism is a life-loving, rational philosophy that millions of people adhere to. Now we're ready for something that goes quite a few steps beyond just explaining our principles. Every revisionist movement needs a set of goals — guidelines that are clear, concrete and that will effect significant changes.

The following Five-Point Program reflects attitudes which allow others to decide whether they wish to align themselves with Satanism or not. Each is necessary for Satanic change to take place. When asked what we're "doing," here's the answer:

1) *Stratification* — The point on which all others ultimately rest. There can be no myth of equality for all — it only translates to mediocrity and supports the weak at the expense of the strong. Water must be allowed to seek its own level without interference from apologists for incompetence. No one should be protected from the effects of his own stupidity.

2) *Strict taxation of all churches* — If churches were taxed for all their income and property, they'd crumble overnight of their own obsolescence, and the National Debt would be wiped out as quickly. The productive, the creative, the resourceful should be subsidized. So long as the useless and incompetent are getting paid, they should be heavily taxed.

3) *No tolerance for religious beliefs secularized and incorporated into law and order issues* — Re-establishing Lex Talionis will require a complete overturning of the present in-justice system based on Judeo-Christian ideals, where the victim/defender has been made the criminal.

Amnesty should be considered for anyone in prison because of his alleged "influence" upon the actual perpetrator of the crime. Everyone is influenced in what he or she does. Scapegoating has become a way of life, a means of survival for the unfit. As an extension of the Judeo-Christian cop-out of blaming the Devil for everything, criminals can gain leniency, even praise, by placing blame on a convenient villain. Following the Satanic creed of "Responsibility to the responsible," in a Satanic society, everyone must experience the consequences of his own actions, for good or ill.

4) *Development and production of artificial human companions* — The forbidden industry. An economic "godsend" which will allow everyone "power" over someone else. Polite, sophisticated, technologically feasible slavery. And the most profitable industry since T.V. and the computer.

5) *The opportunity for anyone to live within a total environment of his or her choice, with mandatory adherence to the aesthetic and behavioral standards of same* — Privately owned, operated and controlled environments as an alternative to homogenized and polyglot ones. The freedom to insularize oneself within a social milieu of personal well-being. An opportunity to feel, see and hear that which is most aesthetically pleasing, without interference from those who would pollute or detract from that option.

This is the encapsulated version of the current thrust of Satanic advocacy. So when somebody asks you, "Well, what do Satanists do?", you will be qualified to tell him. To further explore some of these points, read the following.

This Must Never Happen Again

When a point of critical mass is reached — the point of no return — the "package" it came in will never sell any more. There will always be the clichéd "This Must Never Happen Again." But it takes painful memories and evolutionary strangulation to focus them into an effective warning.

The American Civil War — the destruction of Atlanta, brother against brother, son against father, wreaking carnage on common ground. This must never happen again.

The First World War — mechanized warfare, hometown boys crushed on foreign soil by metal monsters. This must never happen again.

The Second World War — holocausts and nuclear leavings. This must never happen again.

The current Third World War — human locusts overrunning the world, necessitating the thinning out of populations because the Rule of the Fool has, for the first time in history, threatened to destroy civilization and evolution. This must never happen again!

Until space colonies accommodate the teeming, huddled masses, how will this war be resolved?

Technology has left human self-awareness in the dust. Surely, it would be simpler and more economically practical to continue the propagation of consumers at the cost of human evolution. But the earth could not survive. How to isolate and evolve genetically superior humans is the great task of stratification.

Space Ghettos

It has been said we all must become "productive members of society." What society? A universal society? A stratified society? A personally-chosen society? "No," comes the reply from the dictators of acceptability, "the society you live within — when in Rome..." But suppose there's no more Rome in which to do as the Romans? Suppose Rome is no different in most ways — ways that really count — than Hong Kong, Mexico City or Los Angeles?

If stratification means ghettoization, let it be. Call it insularism — whatever you wish. But let's have different rules for different people, providing there are different environments. Regulations imposed upon the dwellers who thrive in a cesspool should not be imposed upon those who have chosen to lead a monastic life. Nor should the restrictions of a monk be imposed on those who prefer to spend their time in the drawing room.

Let's face it — most people are locusts, part of a herd. Herd behavior suits them, and they thrive on it. Through chromosomal and conditional cloning, they cannot be otherwise. The solution is a new kind of ghetto, with its regulations, restrictions, status symbols, incentives and benefits tailored to its inhabitants' needs. Above all, however, it must not be called a "ghetto," even though it occupies most of the land. Mongrelization has produced a very large ghetto, but ghetto it is. Space limitations withstanding, new ghettos will be space ghettos. The desirability of Outer Space migration has made it easy. The herd has been softened up to it by the media since the days of Buck Rogers and Flash Gordon. But please, don't dampen the enthusiasm of these pioneers by the term "space ghetto." Better to refer to it as "new frontiers."

When ghettos become the mainstream of society, islands of individuality cannot help but harbor an elite. And that earthly elite must be sanctioned at any cost.

Destructive Organisms

VANDALS, THOSE WHO DESTROY AND DEFACE OBJECTS AND PROPERTY OTHER than their own, should, when apprehended, be destroyed, or at least punished in a fitting manner. If a painting hanging in a museum is slashed, the perpetrator of that act should be eviscerated. If paint is used to deface, the defacer's countenance should be permanently dyed in an irregular and repellent manner. If a carefully tended shrub or plant is wantonly ripped up by the roots, the culprit's arm should be ripped out of its socket.

No one has the right to harm or destroy another's belongings. Vandalism is seldom motivated by profit or revenge, but simply an urge to destroy. Those who indulge in gratuitous destruction show the same degree of respect for inanimate things as the do for themselves. They cry out by their acts to be destroyed.

Vandalism has for too long been paid scant attention, simply because, "after all, it's only a tree or statue, windshield, schoolroom, or theatre seat." It's assumed these things can be repaired or replaced, unlike crimes involving bodily harm. But the value of a painting which has been slashed should be recognized for more than its monetary worth. Inanimate though it is, the painting contributes far more to others' pleasure — and life itself — than does the living creature who defaces it.

Immunity from punishment goads the vandal to pursue his destructive lifestyle. He is only slightly removed, and often identical in temperament, to the "thrill" killer of animals, who knows that even if he should be apprehended, he'll not draw much of a sentence. The latent killers take out their self-hatred on animals or inanimate objects because, quite simply, they can get away with it. If these destroyers hate themselves so much, proclaiming their uselessness by wanton acts of cruelty to organic or inorganic things, then they make ideal game for which there should be perennial open season.

Clothes Make The Slave

*The consciousness of being perfectly well dressed
may bestow a peace such as religion cannot give.*
— Herbert Spencer

HOW OFTEN HAS BEEN HEARD THE EXPRESSION, "A SLAVE TO FASHION." WHAT
once described a fop or clotheshorse now applies to practically everyone. Fashion in clothing has become a tool with which to create the
type of "police state" dreaded by most as an impending threat to individuality. Ironically, those who fear the worst, the self-professed non-con-
formist, is unwittingly playing right into the hands of the puppet master.
He mistakes mediocrity for individuality, and all the while he laughs at
the past he becomes an unwitting embodiment of the worst kind of contemporary kitsch.

Just as one will pay plenty for a new economy car ("Americans love
economy and will pay anything to get it") so will most conform to whatever clothing standards are foisted upon them, so long as it is accompanied by a convenient rationale. Consider the development of trousers
for women. It came with "emancipation." Even though sexual mores
were becoming looser, women started wearing trousers for their "freedom of movement." Through the 1940s to the present time women have
worn slacks, capris, pedal pushers, and whatever else was in style, so
long as they could spread their limbs in comfort. In so doing they have
established a standard of prudery that would make Victoria look bawdy
by comparison.

Amidst carefully programmed porn, slick and abundant, exists today
a primness unrivaled in Western culture. In their freedom people have
become accustomed to depictions once only accessible to gynecologists
and proctologists. One can purchase all manner of material depicting
human genitalia in its most aseptic glory. Yet try to catch a glimpse of

bare leg on a woman walking down the street. Turn-of-the-century pet-ticoats couldn't do a better job of concealing a nasty ankle or calf so much as a shapeless pair of pre-washed denim. Photo essays abound portraying the labia of emancipated women, but where in public dares a lady display an inch of bare thigh when not swimming, playing tennis or sunbathing? Saint Pantihoes doth protect her upper limbs from the gaze of the heathen.

Lust comes packaged in an instruction book, a sensitivity class, an automated grope session, a chess-like game played by robot-like partici-pants. Homosexuals are the referees. The referees have their own games, but theirs are less often played by robots, for their own rules (which they themselves have made) are the most conducive to unaffect-ed behavior. Sounds contradictory? Not really. Amidst all the plumage, leather, SM, posturing and drag, is an aura of gut-reaction sex. Homo-sexuals have not been duped by the prudes, and are the beneficiaries of heterosexual stupidity and pliability. Homosexuals are the only people who have approached sexual freedom. The rest are more hung-up than ever before, and the sad thing is, they don't know it and would resent any attempt to change their situation.

The growing acceptance of homosexuality (which was needed to decrease the birthrate) manifested its influence on standards of dress and physical desirability. Soon men appeared more feminine and women more masculine, and a monster called "sex differentiation" began to creep forth. By the 60s, classic archetypes of comeliness were reversed. Most likely, the man would make a better woman, feature for feature, and the woman could easily pass for a man if she added a little fake stubble or beard.

The true act of blasphemy is achieved more by violating certain stan-dards of dress than by political dissent, as Herbert Spencer proclaimed. You may think you are protesting social inequity or sexism by wearing poverty-chic or gas station elegance. Patched, faded, ragged, stained, wrinkled or drab. If you can't exercise a keen sense of innovation or re-creation, it may have dawned on you to wear a uniform. Perhaps a frayed and patched mechanic's jumpsuit or some other frayed uni-form of the dehumanized. Who says *1984* hasn't come home to roost?

Babbitt's Last Stand

EVERYBODY LOVES A WINNER. EVERYBODY LOVES A LOSER AS WELL. THE in-betweens, the neglected nonentity known as the middle class, are those who receive no gratuities. A guy with a little money must work like hell to get more. Nobody gives him anything for nothing. If one is cursed by a mediocre lifestyle he can progress only by appearing either more downtrodden than he is or more affluent than he is.

One consantly hears that the middle class pays the bills for society, which is, of course, accurate. The rich get richer and the poor get … richer. The struggler gets nowhere. Religious orders have thrived on contrived poverty by posing as beggars in dire need. Welfare recipients never worry where next month's rent will come from, have cars (but eschew driver's insurance), medical care, color TVs, grass, booze, contraceptives, education, legal aid, food stamps, and more. Furthermore, a destitute appearance frees one from the rigors of good grooming; one can wear rags, go unwashed, sit or lie on floor, ground, or rooftop. No creases need be kept in trousers, grease and dust may decorate clothing, tears and rips may go unmended, food may be spilled over garments, upholstery, and rugs with impunity. Nothing can be stolen that cannot easily be replaced, often by the same method. The slightest talent will soon be recognized amidst austerity and poverty, for there is little glamor to obscure it. The humility implied by this lifestyle attracts aid, sponsorship, and support from those in more affluent circumstances, whose self-esteem is boosted by acts of charity.

The lowest have nothing to lose and everything to gain. When one sleeps on the floor, one need not fear falling out of bed. A pipsqueak can feel like a big shot when he is around those who have less than himself. Then he will react to his feelings of grandeur by patronizing the nonentity, not realizing that his inferior probably has greater security and comfort than himself.

The lowest pay no taxes, are dismissed from jury duty and other public servitude, yet are provided with police and fire protection. No tithings can be extracted from them by religions, yet they are the benefactors of religious charities. If they form the most ad hoc religious body, however, their presumed poverty ensures them cooperation from tax boards, enabling them to extract tax-free plunder from others. They are truly a privileged class.

Because a loser is no threat to anyone, he is an ideal candidate for love and kindness, bestowed in even greater abundance by those who consider weakness a virtue. At the other end of the spectrum, a winner is respected and somewhat feared, and because he is at the top, will find ready supplicants who will do much to curry his favor. To know him, however slightly, lends identification. A popular hero need but hint that he desires something and it will be provided by one who wishes recognition. Those who understand the poseur's need to impress will take full advantage by raising the price. That is why a fool and his money are soon popular but later broke. Whoever can affect a convincing impression of wealth, culture and influence, however, will find many favors bestowed upon him. Others of lesser bearing will not "see him coming" and raise the price, but instead will unconsciously "buy" an ego-gratifying affinity by charging less than normal.

Persons in high circles live by a tacit understanding that money is something to be discussed and displayed to the lower classes, but of little necessity to their own sovereignty. A famous personage will patronize a certain restaurant where an arrangement has been made permitting the celebrity and his entourage free meals in exchange for the use of the celebrity's name in column items, which seldom neglect to mention that he is a big tipper (encouraging social climbers to do likewise). Most importantly, a celebrity's presence adds prestige to any establishment.

There are strong similarities between the bestowal of benefits to both the lowest class and the highest. The public figure gets it free, or rather trades his stature for his gifts which are provided by those who require his presence or sanction, that they might collect from the strugglers. The strugglers pay the rich man's bills as well as the poor's. It may take money to make money, but when money becomes less valuable, other forms of wampum will sustain the adage. It takes creature comforts to accrue additional comforts; power begets power; influence provides greater influence. These things may be obtained with money, but money is not mandatory for their attainment. To obtain and acquire, one must at least present an image of either poverty or affluence.

I foresee a time when the "upper" class will flourish by a sophisticated form of barter while the "lower" class will be provided for by the State, each according to his ability and needs. There will be no "middle class."

If one of the lower class displays upward-motivation with ability, he will discard his dependence upon the State and move to the higher class. Conversely, if a member of the higher class finds discomfort in the impositions made upon him by his peers and surroundings, he will welcome the ordered and dependent life provided the lower class.

In such a society a certain degree of strife must exist. Where the family unit cannot provide it, controlled outside turmoil must be made available. Lest this read like a utopian fantasy, it should be realized that strife and anguish are essential to a utopia since a touch of masochism prevails in the most habitual sadist. A utopia without problems would not be a true utopia, for it would lack the dilemmas and scandals that fill the void of intellectual lethargy and ineptitude.

Gifted Sensitives

MOST OCCULT TYPES WHO CALL THEMSELVES "SENSITIVES" ARE ABOUT AS sensitive as a toilet seat. One who is truly sensitive has increased susceptibility to external stimuli. A sensitive person is self-conscious and often introverted. He or she would lack the colossal gall and assertiveness that characterize those who freely proclaim themselves "sensitives." A few seers through the ages have realized this, and wisely engaged another person as their "front man." John Dee had Edward Kelly and Jeanne Dixon had Ruth Montgomery. One of the pair can then stick to being sensitive while the other takes care of public exposure.

I have found the most highly-touted "sensitives" to be the thickest-skinned, densest, most parsimonious, callous and insensitive specimens of humanity one could encounter. And they are usually stupid as well.

In certain circles it used to be said that if you couldn't get a legitimate job, you could become either a crook or a preacher. Nowadays if a person isn't good for anything else, he can become a pusher or a gifted psychic.

Let Me Entertain You

THERE ARE MANY FINE TECHNIQUES FOR MAINTAINING YOUR IDENTITY AS A Satanist without placing yourself in the role of entertainer. The best method consists of shattering another's cherished preconceptions by a series of disappointments. The result is an uncertainty that is unnerving — and definitely not entertaining. For your victim, that is.

The key is boredom. Most people welcome a challenge. Some will even thrive on insults. There are those who find it stimulating simply soaking up another's presence without a word being spoken. But no one likes boredom.

There is not a single person who is not bored by something. Discover what bores another and you needn't worry that he will vampirize you. Since most people's entire lives are occupied by attempts to relieve boredom, you as a Satanist constitute a tremendous attraction. Whether or not you welcome that attraction is another thing. As you have probably discovered, it has its advantages and disadvantages. How many times have you been trapped into talking Satanism to someone totally uninteresting to you, while the same gathering boasts someone not only receptive but stimulating. Clearly, it is you who is bored and your irresponsible listener who is entertained.

Discourage the pest by boring him more than he bores you. Answer his questions with long rambling narratives that veer completely away from the topic that seems to interest him so greatly. Don't let him interrupt, but insist on finishing your story with apparent enthusiasm with the attitude that he must hear your every word. If he tries to cut in, tell him you'll get to him as soon as you finish your train of thought. There is nothing like an excruciatingly dull and jargon-loaded digression to turn off the most persistent social parasite.

If you are a natural bore but have chosen to become a Satanist in order to compensate for your lusterless personality, read no further.

If you don't want to spend valuable time boring a parasite, employ the element of escape. The sudden phone call, or forgetting to have put money in the parking meter are the more obvious escape mechanisms. A difficult contingency encountered while attempting escape is "just one more question." It's like the caller who won't let you get off the phone even if you tell him the building is on fire. The solution for the problem is found in the Satanic Statement, "Responsibility to the responsible, instead of concern for psychic vampires." A pest shows little responsibility where you are concerned, yet expects it in return. Cut him off with, "I must attend to something — I'll be right back." Leave him and don't return. In other words, lie. Your conscience shouldn't bother you a bit.

With few exceptions, self-help books teach us how to be interesting, attractive, stimulating, acceptable and entertaining. Emily Post and Dale Carnegie are simple variants of *199 Ways To Pick Up Girls*. Most people need instruction on how to secure invitations to parties, let alone be the life of the party. As a known Satanist, you may not be the life of the party, but rest assured, you will arouse no small amount of curiosity and speculation.

Don't entertain Jesus freaks by debating with them. Logic will get you nowhere, nor will quoting scripture. You present a challenge to those convinced of your malevolence. They secretly nourish the hope that you will submit to a long-winded exchange on theology followed by a harrowing display of diabolical blasphemy. Give them nothing. If there are no witnesses, maybe you might want to give them more than they bargained for, but that's another story altogether.

An effective way to deal with "entertain me" types is the put-on. I'm sure many of you have practiced it in varying degrees: describing orgies, human sacrifices, cattle mutilations, etc., to wide-eyed listeners. The problem with the put-on is that the need to believe is so strong, entertainment/fear will linger long after your departure. You will have neither disappointed, bored or disappeared from them. You will still, albeit in a drastic manner, send them away with their cherished fears intact.

But if you employ the put-on method, your quarry will be left feeling foolish, which is almost as unsettling as being bored. After assuring themselves that you will make an entertaining or amusing pastime, they must be left with a feeling that is is they who have provided you with amusement. The formula can be distilled to: Act deadly serious but appear silly. Remember, in our visually-oriented world, looks mean everything. The "convincer" or gimmick to guarantee a feeling of foolishness is what I call "Satanic kitsch."

Decorate a room with the most hokey Halloween bric-a-brac you can find. Make sure the room is red and black. If you can find a day-glo red, so much the better. Fill the chamber with as many obviously plastic artifacts as you can find. Halloween is the perfect time to stock up on rubber bats, plastic pitchforks, and the like. don't forget Jack-o-lantern and black cat cutouts. Remember, if you're a Satanist it's supposed to be Halloween every night.

Above all, while "entertaining," keep a straight face! Evidence absolutely no true sense of humor other than monster movie host puns on a nine-year-old level, just to show you "really do have a sense of humor" as media folks and civilians usually point to others, with a sigh of relief. To start, serve your guest a Bloody Mary with Lugosi aplomb.

Furnishings should be in awful condition. Try to seat your victim in a lumpy armchair with a strategically sprung spring poking his ass. Your position while talking should, naturally, be upon a seedy throne chair. (To construct such a throne, attach doodads like bats and devil heads and skulls to the top and arms of a regular armchair. A dais can be made from a packing crate painted silver and sprinkled with glitter.)

Attire should be incongruous. Wear the most conservative, well-tailored suit you can afford; or if a woman, a tasteful ensemble of good fit and fabric. Your shoes should be as classic and neat as possible. Over the tasteful garments, wear a cape. Not a well-made cape of rich fabric and quality workmanship, but a thin and skimpy model showing creases and wrinkles, crooked seams and at least one loose thread pleading to be pulled. Wear it slightly askew — just enough to be unnerving. If you can keep a straight face, stick some plastic suction cup horns on your forehead while your victim isn't looking.

For background music try Disney's "Sounds of the Haunted Mansion" album or, if you can find it, the Portsmouth Sinfonia's version of Grieg's "Hall of the Mountain King." Don't use the CD or a taped version, as it's more effective to frequently leave your throne to flip the record. Assistants can be employed to advantage, provided that they too can keep a straight face. Your assistants should wear ill-fitting robes (too short or long and droopy) of similar quality and workmanship as your cape. They should stand about looking as sober as is humanly possible while you entertain your victim with "sincere" comments and answers.

Now is the time when you yank the carpet out from under. When your victim has departed but is still within earshot, bellow forth the loudest and most delighted laughter you and whomever may be on hand can produce. Continue your whooping until you are certain your victim has vacated the immediate neighborhood.

I'm aware of the objections to the preceding technique. It might be argued that instead of making your victim feel foolish, he will go away convinced that Satanists are no better than raucous lodge brothers at a fraternal convention, that you don't take your beliefs seriously and therefore aren't worth taking seriously either. You may feel that antics like the aforementioned are a mockery of Satanism and can only undermine the kind of dignity towards which we strive. If improperly performed, a put-on can do more harm than good. That is why it is essential to select a victim who is conspicuously patronizing or condescending; smug, despite his professed "sincere interest." If your victim really has a sense of humor and a discriminating eye, you may be sure that his opinion of you will soar and he'll most likely want to affiliate with you. Don't hold your breath, though. Chances are good your victim is not imbued with that rare sort of perception, and you will have given him exactly what he deserves: ridicule.

It is a terrifying thing when the animals laugh at the hunter. Take a tip from Harlequin and the Joker. If you imitate a fool well, you are not likely to be fooled by others. To be it bluntly, albeit unoriginally: "A fool who knows he is a fool is indeed a wise man."

Insane Ramblings

MYTHS ARE NECESSARY. SO ARE MANMADE DISASTERS. NATURAL DISASTERS bring people together, without need for contrivance. Manmade disasters—wars, plots, scandals, inquisitions, dilemmas of all sorts — like myths — must be contrived, nourished, and above all, self-sustained, for they are essential to man's emotional needs. They are narcotic. The mob requires regular doses of scandal, paranoia and dilemma to alleviate the boredom of a meaningless existence.

What begins as a seedling of reality germinates into a full-blown myth, which in turn picks up constituents along the way who confer substance to it.

One morning in the sixth decade of the 20th century of the common era a sanctified leader was assassinated under circumstances that observers, both learned and casual, were convinced bore political significance. A large-scale conspiracy was presumed. In reality, the Grand Master of a sect of the Knights Templar — an Inquisitor General — engineered the sacrifice in accordance with a tradition demanding a three-fold sacrifice to avenge a grave injustice. The Inquisitor General took the Rites of Hiram seriously, and brooded upon the dynastic rule of Pope Clement and Philip the Fair, which in the 14th century tortured and burned alive the man who held his corresponding office.

The Inquisitor General knew that those who stood for all he despised had caused the death of a fair and exalted damsel — one whose demise had killed more than a small part of his alter-ego. To add insult to injury, the murder of the Angel from the Abyss was sanctioned by one who would usurp his Inquisitor's throne, if permitted. In his mind dwelt the essence of DeMolay, just as others have harbored within themselves the engrams and cellular memory of kindred ones who have gone before. Crazy? Of course. Only small and insignificant men are supposed to harbor such quirks. The great are thought to be immune to folly. The moderately wise man knows different. He knows that we are all crazy, but stronger personalities shelter more elaborate grotesqueries. And the strongest men cry in secret and hurt inside the most. In this entire world of sham and fakery, there is no greater truth.

On that day in the month of November, the monarch whose revels had prompted the death of the exalted damsel rode through the crowd in his papal chariot. The monarch whose rebels were unlike those so charitably attributed to him, and whose gaiety was unbridled. The thronging mob was long amassed before the Green and cap'ring upon the Knoll.

That morn, a secret password moved from lips to waiting ears. A fifth of Hiram Walker for Tubal Cain to toast the Morning Star. A fifth of Hiram Walker was delivered. And a volley of shots rode the wind that tramps the world. And then the rose which had been over one year dead began to bloom anew. Verily, it grew with each succeeding sacrifice until, unrecognized, it might depose the sterile virgin and softly glow as the Rose of the World.

And the Grand Inquisitor, the Emperor of the Hidden Realm, sensed that unfoldment, and bore himself nigh unto the Kingdom of Shadows, that he might culminate his three-fold retaliation. Having wreaked his prime vengeance in Dallas, a time passed until the second tribute was exacted in that very city from where She was taken. And with the second, Azrael came forth from out of the East to bear the sin for the mob. Shortly thereafter, as the Earthlings approached the Moon, a dark portent on that very eve didst verify the third impending doom. A comely maid who deigned to dally with a blighted consort perished 'neath murky waters.

The Grand Master of the Assassins, having witnessed the certitude of his vindication, then departed his office and moved into the Deepest of all Night. And hard by his departure swelled a clamor. And a war ended. Yet still the mob cried for blood.

And now the mouth of my raving approaches its own dear tail and its jaws snap hungrily to grasp that barbed appendage.

"MYTH!" cries the mob. "Give us MYTH!" A still, small voice is heard among them that whimpers, cajoling, "Truth—make the myth be true." But a deafening roar ascends, reiterating, elaborating, "Tell us a scandal — of mafia and CIA! — of Watergates and chaos and assorted crises!" "Of shortages and impeachments and silent deaths by secret means!"

"Frighten us — with depression and inflation and the impending collapse of social structures and economic extinction! Tell us of police states and Cromwell reborn! Terrify us! Worry us! TELL US!"

I have told enough for one night.
The dawn is breaking.
You have had
enough scandal
to think about.

But remember, all this is madness....

Law of the Trapezoid

WE ALL REACT TO WHAT WE SEE. JUST AS SOUNDS AND ODORS INFLUENCE OUR behavior, so do visual patterns and shapes. Some make us feel good. Others disturb us. Whether you like to admit it or not, the fear response is the one most easily aroused. Since self-preservation is nature's highest law, fear motivates. Hence we give our attention first to sensory impressions that represent things that we once, far back in racial memory, feared. Fear is the prime mover.

Fear of failure, fear of lack of recognition, identity, acceptance. Fear of loneliness, rejection, annihilation, the unknown. These persist well after the fundamental fears of starvation, harsh elements, and other more obvious physical fears have been pushed deep into our subconscious. If we did not fear the passage of time and death, nothing much would get done.

Any shape or spatial concept that triggers fear could therefore be considered evil, yet without such "evil," there could also be no progress, only complacency and stagnation. Needless to say, the fearsome is also fascinating and awesome.

What shapes intensify fear? Those which are overbearing, unbalanced, jagged, confusing. The reason a triangle or pyramid in its perfect form is pleasing, is because it is complete, like the imaginary vanishing points in drawings. A lot has been written about Egyptian pyramids. Here is why:

1) They are awesome because they are so big, but are pretty because they are a perfect form.

2) They are Egyptian, and the Egyptians were supposed to be smart fellows.

3) A lot of questions and theories can be connected with them.

Statements #1 and #2 are easy to understand. Statement #3 presents great riddles, like:

Q: Why were pyramids built in that shape?

A: Because they looked good that way and could be built as big as a monarch desired without fear of toppling over.

Q:. Why were they built?

A: Pyramids were the WPA programs of Ancient Egypt. People had to be kept busy during slack periods, and monumental egos had to be served. Had there been radio or TV, smaller monuments would have been built.

Q. What can they tell us?

A. That people were pretty much the same then as they are now.

The way a pyramid looks doesn't really upset anybody, except conspiracy theorists. Put the same shape in a contiguous row and you get an unconsciously scary image, like the teeth of a saw or shark, or the ridge on a dragon's back. The pyramid range also disturbs since it has no single vanishing point. Triangles which are imperfect are also disturbing, especially in groups.

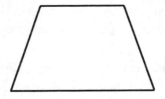

The most disturbing shape of all is a trapezoid in its myriad forms. A perfect trapezoid is a frustrated pyramid. In fact, the place where a pyramid or triangle is lopped off to make a trapezoid is actually called the frustum. A trapezoid says to the unconscious, "I am here, solid as can be, more massive than an ordinary block, but something's missing and it bothers you." Of course, you know what's missing: a triangular top, like the one with the eye on the back of a dollar bill. Don't let that little pyramid with the bright eye fool you. That's to draw your attention away from the real thing: the big trapezoid beneath it. All competent magicians are masters of misdirection and the Masons who designed the seal knew a thing or two.

Angles are space-planes that provoke anxiety — that is, those not harmonious with natural visual orientation — will engender aberrant behavior. Exceptions occur where a sort of reverse polarity exists in a creature: extreme mental imbalance or perversity, or perhaps even extreme rationality and awareness.

I've always been interested in alleged haunted houses, strange places where unease was present, where murders and suicides were frequent, uninhabitable but seemingly innocuous areas and buildings, abodes of consistent failure to dwellers or occupants whose lives had previously been tranquil. Since my earliest years, I've been drawn to such places, curious of their origins and circumstances associated with them. I was fascinated by scenes of Mayan and Aztec temples, of oil-drilling rigs, of trestles and wartime bunkers, of lighthouses and buildings with mansard roofs. And of objects, too: the old-style coffin like an elongated hexagon, the 1936 Cord sedan, the Baguette diamond, the slanted blade breaking the symmetry of the guillotine.

During the course of investigating alleged haunted houses or blighted areas, I soon dismissed the prevailing superstition, i.e., a deceased person's "spirit" restlessly hanging about. It occurred to me that even if a living entity's violent or tragic demise provided a "haunting," perhaps the house itself was the catalyst for their misfortune. It seemed that the physical environment itself played a major role. The place either catalyzed or intensified all acts committed in its precincts.

I was led to contemplate the common denominator that all sites of outré or disturbed behavior possessed. In each case angles were present that violated either topographical or architectural symmetry and perfection. "Comfortable" or psychologically secure configurations were either lacking or subservient to planes that inspired hostility and fear.

I examined files of cases dealing with structures supposedly haunted or cursed with continuing failure, death, financial loss, insanity, fire, tragedy. Many were visually aberrant in the most flagrant manner. Others were not. A mansard roof is de rigeur in every artist's conception of the haunted house. Why did the artists automatically render them in that fashion? Good fairies' castles all were depicted as having peaked towers and gently rounded arches. Jolly elves lived in cottages with rounded corners and cake icing roofs. The good folk dwelt in Graustarkian tranquility in snug and womblike homes with curlicues cut into the shutters. Bluebeards and Frankensteins all lived in stark, monolithic, and grotesquely bastioned abodes. Frankenstein created change and reaction by duplicating God's handiwork.

The architecture of war: medieval storming towers, the martello towers on the English coast, and the latter-day "mystery towers" resting on the sea bottom offshore, the Maginot and Siegfried Lines, the Manzi submarine sheds, pillboxes, bunkers, tank traps, the deflective sloping sides of armored vehicles and turrets, gas chambers, atomic reactors — and the very lavastone marker in the desert where the first atomic bomb was exploded. War creates change.

The mad buildings in the works of the painters of reaction, Breughel and Bosch; the erratic sets in the schauerfilmen of Germany — *Caligari, Nosferatu, Metropolis;* the bizarre staging of Nijinsky's suprahuman capering; the truncated volcanic eminence from which Disney produced Tchort in *Fantasia's* "Night on Bald Mountain;" the architecture of the Bauhaus — of Gröpius and Poelzig — and Frank Lloyd Wright, the long cursed pioneer, whose houseboy went berserk at Taliesin and killed seven persons and set fire to the house, exactly when the construction of Wright's first excursion into trapezoidal design was completed; the ill-fated Midway Gardens resort in Chicago. Art creates change.

The altars of violence and sacrifice: the temples of the Maya and Aztec magicians formed of trapezoids and sustained by the sacrificial blood of the chosen ones, the truncated pyramids upon which hearts were cut from living victims and held aloft and hot to Quetzalcoatl and Hapikern. The same temples made visible in the striations of the Mitchell-Hedges crystal skull. The citadel of Iskanwaya in Bolivia which was autonomously Satanic. The necropoli of skull cults of neolithic cultures — Lepenski Vir in Serbia with every building in the settlement trapezoidal in form, as it was at Hacilar in Turkey and Jericho in Jordan. The same area of the world where the Yezidi towers of Satan beamed forth their influence. And the tower in Lovecraft's *Haunter of the Dark,* wherein the shining trapezohedron beams its influence and the Great Old Ones from the brine harken and send forth their earthly emissary. The literary rites of Huxley and Lovecraft and Orwell and the devastation brought forth by the angles in Frank Belknap Long's *Hounds of Tindalos.* Do the rites, in fact, of Quetzalcoatl and Hapikern and Mendes join the rites, in fantasy, of writers who know not the substance of their own mediumship?

In 1962 I isolated my suppositions and distilled them into what I termed "The Law of the Trapezoid." I had ample evidence that spatial concepts were not only able to effect those who were involved in visual confrontations, but far more insidiously, other parties with whom a viewer came into contact. As in any form of contagion, family, friends, and co-workers are affected by signals of anxiety projected by another. The most tranquil and stoical person can be drawn into a chaotic situation if his surroundings are sufficiently disturbing. Often I discovered that subtle aberrations had a more profound effect than readily-recognizable and overt spatial distortions.

A room, apparently perfect in its rectangular form, would be a habitual scene of violence. Other rooms in the same building would be conspicuous because of their lack of disturbance. The "mad" room would be discovered to have one wall slightly off vertical — a small weight on a string suspended from where the wall and ceiling joined would often rest well away from the baseboard. The other walls might be in perfect alignment. In such cases, I often noticed that the aberrant wall had been painted a different color or wallpapered, the occupant being unconscious of why. An aberrant area in a room might also contain articles or furniture held in less favor than other belongings.

Where an entire building would be blighted, it would either have rooms replete with odd and obtuse angles, useless or impractical ells or nooks — assailing occupants from within — or else an erratic, asymmetrical, or foreboding exterior, affecting those who entered and left the premises on a regular basis or lived in visual proximity. In many examples a structure would appear to be crouching, almost like some strange beast waiting to spring, yet not be seen as such by multitudes. Other buildings hinted at faces.

On the cliffs at the end of Manhattan near the Cloisters is a house that, when viewed from the river, resembles a skull. It is so obvious that any adverse effect is negated, relegating it to a charming eccentricity. Likewise, a wildly distorted house in Beverly Hills known as "the witch's house" is so overt in its grotesquerie that it elicits enthusiasm rather than unconscious revulsion. Contrast such structures with others whose physical aspect is actually disturbing but architecturally orthodox.

The John Hancock Center in Chicago looms like a Martian sentinel in its black splendor, its sloping sides and dark color presenting a brooding spectacle with its twin devil horns/antennae bisecting its top and continuing the frustum up and away into the sky. That its history is already grim is, to me, quite understandable. A newer and far madder building is San Francisco's Hyatt Regency Hotel at the foot of California Street.

The Art Deco treatment of the Golden Gate Bridge provides a streamlined distraction from its hidden angles of unrest and the invisible trapezoid formed by an imaginary line between the towers and each end of the roadbed. With its orange-red color of madness glinting in the setting sun, it has attracted a record number of suicides, rivaled by few other places in the world. I find it interesting that most of the jumpers depart from areas near the bridge towers—the foci of the trapezoid, where its influence from within its precincts is most strongly manifested.

There are objects, too, whose presence in an area continually affects those in attendance. The shape of a piece of furniture, the configuration of a painting, a mural, an appliance, certain "jinxed" automobiles, the angles inherent in all coffins viewing them either from the top (old style) or from the end (new style).

Natural formations in the terrain of land areas or inadvertently aberrant landscaping can cause emotional imbalance and ensuing acts of violence. Anxiety-producing spatial dimension combined with an attendance of disturbed individuals can add up to a wood filled with both psychotics and Reichian DOR (orgone starvation, or life-consuming atmospheric malignancy).

If the Law of the Trapezoid is known, recognized when applicable, and either heeded or utilized, it will save much hardship and tragedy, while still serving as a catalyst for change. Like fire, its powers are twofold, depending on how it is applied. Like the sun, its powers are twofold, depending on whether a thing is growing, grown, or dying. And like the first crystalline fusion of atoms, it will be the beginning and the end, the Alpha and Omega of all matter. Avert your gaze from the pyramids and look to the trapezoid, and you shall be moved.

Two Wrongs Make a Right

IF A WRONG IS GOTTEN AWAY WITH, AND SOMEONE ELSE REPEATS IT AND ALSO gets away with it, a Right is birthed into existence. The Wrong becomes Righter each time it succeeds. Inasmuch as victors always assume historical rights, it can't be any other way. This is not to imply that anything becomes intrinsically noble through repetition, only that successive acceptance of anything confers rectitude.

There is no such thing as "moral" Right. There is only true Right, the balance of the Natural Law, Lex Talionis, versus acquired Right, bestowed by popular consensus and usage (the rules of the Game). Morality is a human invention conferred by the self-serving interests of the sensually impoverished.

We must constantly confront decisions of whether to live by the Law or by the Rules of the Game. Either way will be "Right." Of the two, I always prefer the way of the Law, but it is often riskier and more brutal. The latter — beating them at their own game — requires more planning, time, strategy and money. That's why in all issues enforced by false moralisms and specious Rules of the Game but unfettered by legalities I apply my own rule, which is: "There are no rules."

If you create a new rule and it takes hold, you have made a Right for yourself, however self-serving. Whatever prevails, overwhelms, holds in thrall, disarms, terrifies, frightens, controls, constrains, enslaves, or otherwise contributes to man's masochistic needs will always be accepted as Right. No amount of lip service to the contrary can eradicate what the past has proven, and the present intensifies.

If a thing or an act is naturally Wrong, a Satanist will try, albeit secretly, to lend Nature a helping hand — as circumstance permits.

Summertime

SUMMERTIME AND THE LIVING IS LOUSY. I HATE SUMMER. AND I'M NOT ALONE. Summertime in urban areas is riot-time, tourist-time, pollution-time and psycho-time. In rural areas it's mosquito-time, sunburn/heatstroke-time, pollen-time, litter-time, boredom-time, vandal-time and gangbang-time. There's no worse time for tragedy than the sticky heat of summer, or for frantic attempts at pleasure. Christmas "joy" is an odious duty, but summer "gaiety" is a maladroit ritual performed with calculated chaos. Persons of refinement prefer the other seasons, which progress through their days less heavy-footedly. Despite nature's tantrums during other seasons, be they storms, floods, ice or snow—man has made summer his personal disaster season. Taking the warmth nature has provided, he has fashioned for himself an environment where his mindlessness flourishes most. It is the only season which validates slobs. Those who have found civilized behavior repugnant the rest of the year can celebrate their boorishness in grand style. I would enjoy spring more were it not for the impending plague of summer with its human locusts thriving in an atmosphere far deadlier (if radiation levels are considered) than the worst blizzards. Other seasons may be violent in themselves, but summer is virulent, an incubator for personal malaise and discord. I like autumn and winter best. A sunny autumn day has a relaxed purity, a mellow tranquility. As with the ancients, my autumn runs from August through October, and winter, from November to February. My favorite aspect of summer is that on the Solstice the days finally grow shorter and the nights longer. The best thing about any day is its gentle lapse into night, the dark mantle whence all secrets evolve. Winter time is hell for many, and understandably. It's a Tartarus that causes havoc. But within a snug harbor, winter can be the great season of contrast.

In my noir world, the sticky glare of summer has no place, save for those parts of the world where nature has cheated humankind by injecting regional and regular fog and rain. An ardent supporter of controlled environments, many years ago I fashioned a room, a true ritual chamber, which I call The Cornell Woolrich Memorial Hotel Room. It could as easily have been named The Weegee Room or The Reginald Marsh Room. It consists of an exact duplication of a seedy hotel room in an old but still sound brick building. The walls are papered with faded yellow daisies and a bluish carpeting clashes pleasantly with the brindle colored woodwork. Outside the single window it is always night and always raining, and an intermittent flash of a neon sign pulsates, and on a butt-scarred mahogany bureau an old veneered radio plays songs of lost love and after-the-war dreams. The wood-grained metal bed upon which I rest bears the inevitable chintz spread, and a nightstand supports a lamp and ancient portable typewriter. And the artwork; framed prints of sad flowers trying to look cheery, a musty landscape with leaden sky, the casino at Catalina island, and a Moran cowgirl sitting on the corral fence. A few clothes (vintage) hang on wire hangers on wire hooks, and on one dangles the obligatory shoulder holster. Above all, the fragrance of every such room that ever was mingles with the sweet scent of the wet pavements beyond. I have shown this room to a few. The famous or notorious love it and understand it, and want to spend a night or more. The pretentiously unaware are repelled, sickened, and cannot get out soon enough, which suits me fine.

> *The mind is its own place, and in itself*
> *can make a Heav'n of Hell, a Hell of Heav'n*
> — John Milton, *Paradise Lost*

How to Become a Werewolf
The Fundamentals of Lycanthropic Metamorphosis; Their Principles and Application

ANYONE IS A POTENTIAL WEREWOLF. UNDER EMOTIONAL STRESS CIVILIZED human qualities regress to basic animal reaction, and a threshold of potential physical change is reached.

Temperament

People who normally behave in a coarse and boorish manner would be thought to be bordering on an animal state, hence making a complete transition relatively effortless. This is a fallacy, for churls consider themselves as humans the highest and most noble form of life. They are *almost* animals *all* of the time, so they dare not "go over the brink," for that would be abhorrent.

One who has only risen to the curbstone dares not return to the gutter. Only the higher man can metamorphose, as his ego will allow him to go all the way. He knows he is circumspect and cultured the greater part of his life. So a transition to animalism can be entertained without compunction. Manifestations of this phenomenon are abundant. The most polished individuals become the most degraded when the proper opportunity presents itself. There is no drunk quite so sloppy as a rich drunk. Analogies of such polarities are endless: drunk as a lord, Dr. Jekyll and Mr. Hyde, Count Dracula, Jack London, etc. In virtually every literary, stage or motion picture treatment, the lycanthrope is in his normal state depicted as a human of warmth, understanding, sensitivity and intelligence.

The three principal emotions of sex, sentiment and wonder may be considered as triggering mechanisms, as will be shown by the following formula by which one can effect the change from man into beast.

Environment

Everyone has at some time or other wandered into an area of such foreboding that it is felt that someone or something is lurking in the shadows, watching, ready to spring and devour. Perhaps it was a deserted house, perhaps a lonely path through the trees, possibly an abandoned quarry. In many cases it is known or discovered that such areas have witnessed death of an unexpected or unusual nature, or perhaps mayhem, rape, or other violence. All actions involving intense or increased production of adrenaline on the part of either victim or perpetrator (lust, terror, aggression, defense, etc.) is followed by detumescence in the form of varying degrees of receptivity (shock, total submission, unconsciousness, death, etc.).

The polarity that such an atmosphere has undergone can be likened to an area where heavy concentrations of electricity have accumulated and discharged repeatedly, thereby recycling the ionization of the atmosphere in a chaotic and disturbing manner. The initial 'charge' and attraction of such an area proceeds from its spatial and geometric pattern. This can be likened to an existing feeding trough to which animals come from miles around and dine on the carcasses of their predecessors.

The sado-masochistic dichotomy, with its needs for expression, keeps such an area well-stocked with both hunters and hunted. The hunted are drawn to such a spot because of the frightening yet submissive thrill obtained from the environment. Predators then come forth, drawn by the ideal hunting conditions and abundance of game. Often, however, the hunters have not originally entered the preserve as hunters, but as fear-inspired searchers after thrills.

If this appears far-fetched, consider a phenomenon common to children on Halloween or on any other night where the setting is right. The child deliberately goes out expecting to be scared, succeeds in being scared, then considers how much fun it might be to scare others, once he has been purged of his fear-needs. He then becomes the hunter and the next child who comes along is his quarry. The entire phenomenon is akin to a recognized psychological manifestation of those who outwardly fear a situation while at the same time doing all in their power to encourage its occurrence.

Preparation

This children's Halloween game gives us the clue to the role change necessary in lycanthropic metamorphosis. Briefly, it is thus: Enter the area you know to be trauma-producing with the fullest intention of being frightened. Allow yourself to be frightened. If necessary wear articles of clothing conducive to the most submissive or vulnerable image. "Accidental" victims are always thus attired. Get the feel of the place as a victim, allowing yourself to be frightened as much as you can. If you can supplement your fear with a sexually stimulating feeling, so much the better. Allow yourself to virtually shake apart with fear and if possible attain an orgasm by whatever means may be necessary, for this will make your subsequent lycanthropic changeover easier.

After you have released all fear and fled the scene of your terror/ecstasy, go home and ruminate over what you felt. You will soon discover that a sort of magnetic pull will manifest itself, beckoning you back to the blighted spot. This uneasy attraction will increase with each succeeding day, ideally bordering on compulsion. When you find yourself unable to resist the temptation to return to your danger spot, repeat the first incident in much the same manner. You will find the second foray into the area even more profound than the first, due to the anxiety and anticipation that has developed over the past days.

In the truest sense, you have been performing a ritual of sending forth your energy into a living, breathing environment. That environment, because, of continual taxation upon its vitality, acts as a vampire, absorbing energy from those it attracts and, once having attracted, contagiously ensnares for future sustenance. Wilhelm Reich called such areas DOR, indicating a persistent starvation of orgone or enervation of the atmosphere. Such areas are atmospherically hungry and in their barrenness cry out to be fed. All alleged haunted house and terror spots are reinforced by the accumulation of energy supplied them by the anxieties of occupants and anticipation of visitors to return, i.e., the obsessive thoughts of those who have been affected.

The second time you enter your chosen area, you may not be able to spend as much time as the first, owing to your increased fear and subsequent need to quickly exercise/exorcise it and remove yourself. At this point you are prepared for the metamorphosis — unless you find the second time a "charm," and crave to entertain your fears to greater and more ecstatic heights, in which case you either haven't scared yourself enough, or else there is little chance for role-change. In other words, before you can become the hunter, you must first have aroused and then exorcised a need to be the victim.

If you are a habitual "victim" it is wise to proceed with caution. Your desire to be frightened and its ensuing manifestations could impel you into a situation whereby you could be severely injured or killed. If, however, you are able to meet your fright-needs and exorcise them, then go on to the next step:

Metamorphosis

Attire yourself in a manner conducive to the change that is to be effected. Legends of Berserkers donning the skins of wolves and bears hold substantial meaning, in view of the importance of costume in ritual. Dress in the most stereotyped, "corny" manner, as the second skin that you wear is a potent element in complete transmogrification. This is hermetic or sympathetic magic exemplified (as above, so below). If you wear the mask of a wolf or the skin of a beast, it is preferable if it is not genuine, as you can better infuse a facsimile of the chosen animal with your own personality, while drawing from the known attributes of the species represented. The skin or mask will serve as a catalyst, a blueprint, for what you will become as you merge with it.

Enter the blighted area with eager anticipation. When you approach the spots where you would have previously been the most frightened, allow yourself to revel in the thought of how terrifying it would be to another if they were to feel the same fear you had felt, plus the added terror with an actual manifestation of an unfamiliar and grotesque creature. In short, it is now your role to contribute to the fearsomeness of the place.

The stage has been set and all necessary components have been activated. You have experienced intense fear, now it is your turn to manifest intense fearsomeness in the form of bestiality. Allow yourself to slouch, almost dropping down on all-fours at times. Children are quite proficient in their approximations of animals. Remember when? You've also romped on all-fours with a dog or cat, no doubt. Did you ever consider the implications?

Sniff the air, savoring it and the smells of the environment in which you stand. If there are trees around, get close to them, touching them, pawing them, climbing and shaking them. Do everything possible to emulate an animal. If you are in a building, urinate against a wall or on the floor. Remember, wild creatures are not housebroken! Snort, snarl, roar, grunt — make all the unsavory sounds you want.

As you progressively become more imbued with the sensation of being an animal, you will actually feel certain areas of your body responding in a manner alien to the human anatomy. Your legs will become haunches. Your arms will become forelimbs for claws or paws that crave to grasp at the nearest thing. Your countenance will change. Your facial muscles will begin to twitch in bestial grimaces. All of your senses will become more acute. You will feel the need to urinate more frequently. You will become fascinated with the moon, especially if it is full. If you are indoors, you will seek to explore behind things, into cracks, below boards. You will feel a desire to snuffle into closed areas, burrowing your head and body.

If you feel sexual desire, it will be in a rapacious manner, and if you should perceive another person who might not normally appear sexually to you, the nature of your transformation will make up for their lacking attributes. The impulse to attack will be present, but your higher mind must refrain, taking over and holding you in your spot, while still allowing you sufficient impetus to release yourself. This is the stage of transformation where control is essential, unless one is with a willing partner who can enter the Game as the hunted and revel in their roles. If this is the case, then complete sexual assault can be manifested. If not, sufficient restraint to attain sexual release without an attack upon the "victim" must be exercised.

At the moment of orgasm, a complete and irrevocable encompassing of the animal within must occur, with whatever abandon to this level may ensue. It is at this tune that the change will take place, and if one should be unfortunate (or fortunate?) enough to witness your metamorphosis, you may be assured they will never forget it.

This entire principle, carried out in a ritualistic exercise between pre-cast hunter and hunted is, of course, the basis of such children's games as hide and seek, where one child revels in being frightened while the other delights in terrifying, often with both roles interchanged within a single episode of the game. As children are naturally closer to an animal state, so they are well qualified to teach us means by which we might bring ourselves closer. It is the transitional nature of children that makes them ideal teachers.

Once your transformation has been effected (remember, the most profound manifestation can only occur after sufficient build-up), allow yourself to "come down," having retreated if necessary to a place where you can unconcernedly drop to the ground or floor. If you have done your exercise well, you should, upon returning to your normal state, feel the desire to partake of nourishment.

The tremendous build-up and discharge of energy in reaching this state will have consumed a vast amount of calories. So the obvious epilogue to your ritual, and completion of the animal cycle, is to eat your fill and go to sleep.

Time to Start Kicking Ass

LEST WE FORGET, SATAN IS THE ACCUSER, THE CHALLENGER OF MOLDY OPINION and tiresome concepts. In its senescence, Christianity seems to be pulling all its old chestnuts out of the fire and creating the most irrational witch hunt ever. Hysteria is not only heeded, but encouraged. Indeed, one wonders about the unquestioning gullibility of not only the general public but specifically those in positions of authority.

Children are enticed — not by Satanists, but by authorities, to concoct damaging lies about their own parents. Any star, circle, triangle, hexagram or octagon becomes a "Satanic" symbol. The list of accursed objects grows: stained glass, ceramic cats, a solid color bathrobe, leather clothes, rock recordings (especially if played backwards). If a *Satanic Bible* is discovered, it becomes proof that its reader perpetrates every crime known to man.

If the foregoing lies are challenged and exposed, the hysteric will declare that the exonerated Satanist is not a real or "classical" (read: Christian) variety Satanist, who steals babies, molests and kills children, and chops up animals. The nuts who indulge in the foregoing are repressed hysterics relating wild masturbatory fantasies or jive artists posing as Satanists in order that they may be "converted" and earn an early parole. "Organized groups" can never seem to be found because of their "secrecy." Nor can the bodies of their "sacrificial victims." But how they try — oh, how they try. A new profession has appeared, the "specialist in the research of the Satanic and the occult," actually, a fancy new name for a hellfire and brimstone preacher. Anyone can hang out his or her shingle as one of these "experts," though, of course, it's more impressive if an insecure asshole has a few letters after his name to prove he is an authorized, accredited liar.

Fear of Satanism is a good way to spice up an otherwise dull and unproductive life. If they can't feel important, at least they can feel righteous in their gutless crusade against a fashionably fiendish enemy.

By bringing Satanism to the millions, the most strident and mindless elements from the ruins of Christianity are showing their faces. They are the worst that traditional religion can produce. Now it's time to kick some ass. These remnants of festering Christianity have attempted to place us in a defensive position, when it is our position to demand answers for their irrational behavior. The antics of Satan-baiters can only succeed in obscuring the socially redeeming qualities wrought by Christianity's two thousand year venture. They have not succeeded in giving Satanism a bad name; quite the contrary, it is Christianity they are besmirching.

We do not molest children or sacrifice animals. But it's open season on the kind of creeps who accuse us of doing so. For them, torture is too sweet.

For centuries, Satanism has been a paper tiger, a smokescreen, a straw man, perpetuated for the vested interests of Christian dogma. Never before had organized Satanists come forth to challenge the convenient falsehoods. Sure, there were the Devil's advocates — Tom Paine, Ben Franklin, Shaw, Twain, London, Wells — but they posed little threat to Christianity as a whole. But when you get many thousands of kids cheering real Satanic symbols and giving the sign of the horns — now that's a real threat! When a book written by a Satanist, for Satanists, is read, translated, and re-read by millions — now that's a threat!

The squealing Christian creep is correct in assuming Satanism is dangerous. It's plenty dangerous but not because of orgies, infant stealing, animal mutilation or other unimaginative titillations. Satanism is dangerous because it encourages originality over herd mentality. Large masses of people who all act and think within a prescribed set of options are much easier to control. And exploit.

Satanism is dangerous in that it encourages strong relationships between two people rather than mechanical adherence to programmed group activity. Loyalty to a mate or friend — even a pet — is more dangerous to a despotic regime than enthusiasm for "causes." Satanism is dangerous for the economy in that it advocates conservation of enjoyable and useful artifacts of the past rather than acquiring the new for newness's sake.

The frantic little Christian believes heavy metal is dangerous because it is a convenient target for his hysteria. It's easy to single out Black Sabbath, Motley Crue, Twisted Sister and all the rest for asinine commentaries, but what about the Satanic music of Liszt, Wagner, Saint-Saens, Beethoven, Mussorgsky, Paganini, Mendelssohn? Perhaps warning stickers are in order for the works of Cole Porter, Rogers and Hammerstein, Jerome Kern and Irving Berlin, whose "Stay Down Here Where You Belong" features a good guy Devil proclaiming, "You'll find more hate up there than you will down below." And what about such tunes as "Get Thee Behind Me Satan," "Old Devil Moon," "Satan Takes a Holiday," "Perfidia," "Temptation," "Taboo," and lest we forget, Frankie Laine or Edith Piaf belting out Shanklin's "Jezebel." Songs that you can understand, lyrics you can hear. If a performer were to do a "new" performance of "Jezebel" or "Stay Down Here Where You Belong" at a rock concert, it could precipitate a Satanic revolution.

I must now address the fear of Satanists who view the new Dark Age with trepidation or alarm. Look to our own past influence and future potential to recognize our power. Consider the air time allocated to evangelists. One can turn on the TV at any time of the day or night and receive overtly Christian (read: anti-Satanic) propaganda. On a lesser level are the investigative reports (anti-Satanic), dramatic fictional presentations (anti-Satanic), "factual" news coverage (anti-Satanic) and "spiritually uplifting" specials (also anti-Satanic). Radio time and printed media are no different. The lower the class of audience, the more irrational the pitch.

As bait or a "grabber," Satanism is iconographically employed with formulaic regularity, like a picture of Marilyn Monroe. (When in doubt, whack the slobs with MM or Satanism.) What might happen if Satanism were given the media time enjoyed by our detractors? Or even a tiny fraction thereof? How often have I seen my own image used as a lead-in to an exploitative television segment or article bearing no resemblance to the concepts I have set forth in no uncertain terms. One must literally stumble upon the *Satanic Bible* in order to absorb Satanism in its true form. The greatest threat of Satanism is when the truth of it becomes known. If a regularly scheduled Satanic TV show were aired, it would wipe out the flannel-mouthed evangelists overnight. We hold a power so fearsome that it cannot be afforded a voice.

Yes, the power is in our hands. We are, more than ever, the accusers. Remember, it is our position, our role to serve as tribunal to those who pretentiously play-act as nemeses. The thought of answering their "accusations," of defending our position, must become an absurdity. Let's put them to the test. Let's interrogate. Let's demand the whys and wherefores of their silly hysterics. We must scourge unreason with inquisitorial intensity. And show them the ridicule they deserve. We are what their old teachers didn't anticipate. There is nothing in their rule-books that can contend with real devils that do not succumb to mythic banishments.

It's open season. That's it.

The Merits of Artificiality

MAN CAN BE EASILY FOOLED. IN FACT, HE HAS SHOWN EVERY INDICATION THAT he *must* be fooled. He complains, "It's a Barnum and Bailey world, just as phony as it can be," yet he won't have it any other way and seems to survive best under the most artificial conditions.

Only when one can fully accept artificiality as a natural and often superior development of intelligent life can one have and hold a powerful magical ability. Artificiality is more than completely honest; it forestalls disappointment at thing not being what they appear to be. If you know something is phony from the outset, your imagination can make it as real as needs be. But it does require imagination. Believe it or not, everybody has imagination to some degree.

Granted, it doesn't take much imagination to be fooled, either by yourself or someone else. But imagination is taken into the realm of creativity when you infuse the unreal with a reality which will be satisfying. Masturbation is the closest most people ever get to that stage. Unlike the theologies which are dependent upon faith, which raises the debatable into reality, masturbation is based on act that few can contest: sexual exchange. Knowing full well that masturbation is "pretend" does not eradicate its practice. In fact, the selfish nature of masturbation has been shown to produce more intense orgasms than the "real thing." What then becomes the real thing, where orgasm is concerned?

It has been argued that masturbation can become habitual and dull or even negate healthy relationships with real people. Well, I'm damned glad I didn't stop, judging from some of the sorry specimens touted as sexy in recent years. I've never been disappointed by my fantasies.

I'm not antagonistic towards women to whom nature has been unkind in the looks department. I love them dearly. I eschew women who deliberately make themselves physically drab so they will be appreciated for their minds and not viewed as objects. They are as off-base as men who go overboard in their pursuit of seemingly masculine electives, believing that any sign of culture or sensitivity will mark them as pansies. A man can be very strong and resourceful, and still be gentle and sensitive. A woman can be physically glamorous as well as physically capable and mentally advanced.

But what of the urges in the loins of millions who know better but yield to inferior people because, visual animals that they are, plumage means a lot? They wind up enmeshed in dreary relationships because they are constantly trying to fool themselves into believing their mate is either more capable or intelligent than he or she really is. If they could have only begun a relationship with sexual needs as the prime factor, and not pretend that anything more would exist, they could more carefully evaluate genuine quality in another.

Sex is exciting, but companionship is often more meaningful, especially for women. How many women seek companionship with men who have little or nothing to offer other than physical presence? That is surely social masturbation.

Many of you have known of the Church of Satan's goal to develop and promote the manufacture of artificial human companions. Movies and television have been priming the pump for years for a development as inevitable as the automobile or airplane.

Individuals throughout history have sculpted or pieced together physical likenesses of humans, but have done so as automata usually accompanied by music and constructed for eccentric aristocrats. As an art form, contemporary sculptors like Duane Hansen, John deAndrea, George Segal and others have exhibited to shocked and gradually accepting audiences. PVC "love dolls" have proliferated in the back pages of men's magazines, and always with a plain brown wrapper approach. The Church of Satan is the first organization to pull together the threads on one of the major industries of the future.

The taboo against androids for companionship has persisted largely due to the Frankensteinian or Pygmalionistic "imitation of God" trauma. This reason, more than any other, has impeded major manufacturers from proceeding with such a venture. Other economic factors must be considered as well. The purchase of automobiles, electronic leisure products and other "status" purchases will diminish when artificial people become more impressive than the real ones the consumer has usually tried to impress.

We as Satanists can really throw a curve to expectation when answering the usual, "What is Satanism all about?" with "We manufacture artificial human beings," followed by, "In a few years you'll have at least one living with you." You can counter the "Oh, no I won't!" with a wry smile and a "We'll see…" knowing full well that you're a prophet in your own time. I can assure you that peoplemaking requires a lot more imagination, skill, patience and resourcefulness than rewriting the Enochian Keys or preparing for an authentic Babylonian lust ritual.

Not long ago one of my close associates mused, "I wonder what some of our members will come up with in the way of innovation on their own, once the cat is let out of the bag. Can you imagine a convention of Satanists, all accompanied by a humanoid of their own creation?" I must admit, that would create some real speculation other than the tired "Devil worshipping" thing.

The field is so fresh, so wide open for development and experimentation, that a Satanist with some background in arts, crafts, computers, electronics, mechanics, woodworking, plastics, sewing, etc., can readily become a pioneer in a unique field. What can you do to help? Experiment on your own and let us know about it by way of descriptive text regarding materials and construction techniques, accompanied by photos. If enough Dr. Frankensteins put their minds together, a better product will evolve.

In today's world the creation of replacement or supplementary human beings is the most Satanic activity possible. This is not meant as a replacement for the philosophy of Satanism as outlined in *The Satanic Bible*. It is a contemporary vehicle for it.

The Construction of
Artificial Human Companions

THE MEANS BY WHICH A HUMANOID MAY BE CONSTRUCTED ARE AS DIVERSE AS
the choice of materials will allow. In the past, artificial human beings
were fashioned of metal, the sections of the body joined as in a suit of
armor, or else were formed of rubberized cloth or actual rubber
stretched over a skeletal framework. The mechanism actuating the robot
was contained inside.

The most rudimentary android need be nothing more than convinc-
ingly visual and tactile substitutes. There is nothing wrong with this, as
the prime appeal of the humanoid lies in its approximation of the purchaser's "other half." As nature has intended us to fall in "love at first
sight," that which is most enthusiastically seen will be enthusiastically
accepted. Artificial companions that are pleasingly heard, smelled and
felt also constitute positive selling points. But that an artificial companion looks right is of primary importance.

In such a new industry there is no immediate need for planned
obsolescence, as the opportunity for constant improvement remains
fresh and untapped. As competition between humanoid-producing fac-
tories develops, so will greater elaboration and intricacy of the android.

Initially there will be some reluctance to admit to the use of
androids, especially on the part of persons who most need them. Hence
concealability should be considered in the initial development of
humanoids. Despite the ads one sees of actually grotesque inflatable
dolls accompanying gentlemen to the swimming pool and parties, it is
doubtful whether the egos of the purchasers reached by such ads have
actualized that level of public insouciance, practical jokers excepted.
Many early androids will undoubtedly be relegated to the bureau drawer, foot locker, or space under the garage workbench when not in use,
to be brought out "when the coast is clear."

Before embarking on the project of building a humanoid, consideration should be given to the maker's requirements, needs for secrecy,
and available talent and materials. If you want companionship of a
purely visual nature, techniques employed by modern sculptors can be
utilized. Figures may be carved of wood, styrofoam blocks cemented
together, or cast or molded in the many varieties of plastics available. If
you choose this method, several good books on the market provide
instruction on carving figures in wood and sculpting with various plastic
resins and fiberglass. Papier-maché, plaster, and other methods are easily learned. The main disadvantage of making your android from such
materials is lack of pliability and softness, along with a limitation of
body movement. At worst, you will spend a great deal of time on a creature that is essentially a display mannequin when completed.

If your requirements are largely voyeuristic, you will save much time
by obtaining a discarded or damaged mannequin to use as a base upon
which to build. Mannequins are generally cast from living persons, but it
is unlikely that you will find one ideally suited to your esthetic demands.
Most are extremely thin, so as to best display clothing, and many are
abnormally lengthened in the torso, legs, arms, and neck. Male mannequins are invariably thinner than normal to facilitate dressing them.
Women's faces tend to be aquiline or sterile, and men's bland. No store
wants a seductive-faced woman or compelling-faced man in its window
detracting from the clothing hung upon them. Unless your taste runs to
string beans in women and fashion plates in men, you will have to modify any mannequin.

Though a mannequin makes a suitable base, its movements are usually limited to rearrangement of arms and hands. I have found that
because parts are interchangeable (arms, hands, upper and lower halves
of the body), spare parts add to the flexibility of positioning. My earliest
humanoids were constructed from mannequins which I sectioned, cutting pieces out of legs, arms, necks and torsos, rejoining them with
fiberglass or Celastic, and then adding a compound of resin and talc
over areas built up with various materials. In this manner I created some
grotesque and beautiful people — just like real folks.

If you are content to limit your artificial humans to purely visual
companionship, it doesn't matter how stony their surface. It can be

painted, depending upon your ability, as realistically as any living being might appear.

If you want to shake hands with your creation or give it a little squeeze, however, you'd better have a highly developed imagination or your bubble will burst. Flexibility and tactile realism are obvious improvements on rigidity. There are three basic methods I have employed to achieve these ends: a skin filled with air, a skin filled with stuffing and a molded substance which is soft to the touch.

Let us consider the type purveyed by sex-aid mail order firms featuring advertisements of what appear to be ravishingly glamorous creatures. The purchaser excitedly opens his package to discover a thin vinyl (PVC, not BVD) suit of long pink underwear with a stiff mask attached to its top. He tremblingly unpacks the plastic leotard and finds a valve into which he proceeds to blow until dizzy from hyperventilation. And he is rewarded with what appears to be a thalidomide hydrocephalic glamour girl. Any resemblance to a voluptuous damsel is purely mental. Some models sport a vaginal orifice (or plastic watch-pocket) between the thighs — or other "improvements."

If you want to make your own inflatable companion you can do a better job by cutting vinyl sheeting with a combination tool that both slices and electrically welds a seam in the desired location. To get a reasonable figure, pin the vinyl on a live model much as a dressmaker would, marking where the seams, joints and darts will be. Remove the pins (make sure they are outside the lines you have marked or you'll have leaks) and cut and weld the vinyl. The problem areas of this type of construction are head, hands and feet. The head and neck must be constructed separately, then fitted as snugly as possibly into the neck opening of the vinyl skin and glued with plastic cement to ensure an airtight seal. If you attempt to make the head by the same method as the rest of the figure, it will look like either a hydro- or microcephalic. The same with hands and feet. They will either resemble picnic hams or tiny flippers. Stop construction at the wrists and ankles and insert rigid ankles and feet in addition to separate hands fitted and joined at the wrists. These can be cast from life or salvaged from a mannequin. Seal the joints as you did with the neck. If you're careful the joints will be barely detectable, as vinyl sheeting is extremely thin. In a convenient place (I prefer the back of the neck, as a wig will cover it) place the valve used for inflation either by electric welding or plastic cement used to repair beach toys. Any toy department will yield an inexpensive inflatable toy from which the valve may be removed.

Don't be discouraged if your first attempts don't meet with your expectations, as experimentation and innovation will be your best teachers. The main disadvantage of the inflatable android is its inability to remain in any fixed position due to the equal distribution of air within. The human body is comprised of diverse degrees of density and muscle tone, not to mention an ingenious framework known as a skeleton. Tendons hold limbs and surfaces taut and weight is suitably distributed for human actions. The next method of construction, a skin filled with stuffing, allows for some of these factors. Its main disadvantage is its lack of concealability. An inflatable doll can be stored in a small box, drawer, or carried about in a shopping bag until needed — an attribute real people lack. A stuffed figure takes up as much space as a bonafide human. Unlike the hard-surfaced mannequin type, it is flexible enough to compress somewhat, but nonetheless must be reckoned with if you are worried about storage facilities. A stuffed android can be constructed with or without a skeleton, though an internal framework will eliminate the unnatural stasis inherent in an inflated product.

A basic skeleton may be constructed from dowels or metal or plastic tubing. Joints for hips, elbows, knees, etc., may be fashioned by slotting and pinning or with commercially available ball and socket joints. Two hangers approximating shoulders and pelvic region may be cut from wood, from which arms and legs are suspended. Marionette construction techniques are invaluable and should be studied, as should, of course, human anatomy. I have found that the most easily obtained and efficient substitute for a spinal column is a length of flexible tubing such as is used for gooseneck lamps or electrical conduit. One end is fixed to the pelvis board and the top end goes through the shoulder board right up into the head. Thus the torso and head may be positioned in any manner desired.

The outer skin may be any type of material that can be sewn or glued, like electrically welded vinyl sheeting. Vinyl lacks the resiliency of human skin, however, that either rubber sheeting or stretch fabrics provide. Cut the pattern for the upper torso separate from the lower torso and legs. As with the inflatable doll, forget about the head and hands until later, as these can be problem areas. Close the neck and wrists with a sleeve-like extension to which will be added the head and hands. As with inflatable humanoids, I have found it best to insert rigid pre-formed feet and ankles. When constructing a stuffed figure, this must be done before the stuffing is inserted, pushing the feet, which are attached to the ends of the calf "bones," into the outer skin, which has been formed much like the feet of children's sleepers. I have used a zipper (or velcro) to fasten the two body sections together at the waist. This method not only allows greater ease of stuffing both sections, closing the zipper gradually until the proper amount of stuffing has been inserted, but provides access to the innards of your creation, should you wish to add various "organs," either simple or sophisticated. It is amazing what can be accomplished using a little ingenuity.

Faces can be cast from live persons using established moulage procedures. A flexible latex mask can be laced to a faceless head, the wig concealing the laces. Thus if you tire of one face or basic expression, you can simply replace it with another as easily as tying your shoes. If your dream man or woman is not available for casting, sculpt him in clay, make a cast, and search no more. Wigs can either be pinned to the head or fastened with double-sided adhesive tape or velcro.

Plastics, which are highly toxic if worked by a hobbyist with limited facilities for ventilation, may be employed under industrial conditions. However, open or closed cell flexible polyurethane foam is easily available in sheet or block form, and can be realistically employed as "flesh." Either wrap your armature or skeleton with it or laminate entire blocks and carve with an electric knife. The finished body can be given a "skin" of PVC applied with double-sided tape or covered with a suitable body stocking.

Electronics can easily be incorporated. Voice mechanisms are no challenge whatsoever. I have concealed small recorders into heads with the speaker opening under the wig. Pre-recorded cassettes inserted into a slot under the hairline provide a convincing audible effect.

Odors associated with humans are simple to provide, using perfumes, colognes or worse.

An entire congress of penises, vulvas, vaginas, scrotal sacs, breasts, nipples, etc., may be found in any sex goods store or catalogue. With few exceptions, they are all disembodied. Let us rejoin them to the human forms where they belong.

I have great respect for those who pioneer their own artificial human companions, crude as they might initially be. They will have come a small step closer to playing God and creating man or woman according to their desired image. With a creative outlet as cloaked in age-old taboo as this, innovation may now run rampant — more so than any artform man has yet known.

The bizarre twilight world of the ventriloquist, the puppet-master and the dollmaker can perhaps be understood through other than the minds of psychologists. The acceptable schizoid element in all of us — the one that selects our mates — has a fresh, new, open portal to pass through. Through surrogates the race will survive.

Misanthropia

H. L. MENCKEN SAID, "I RESERVE THE RIGHT TO BE A LONELY MAN." I DON'T crave companionship. It stands in my way. I live for pleasure. There are few persons who can give me as much pleasure as those acts I perform myself. I would rather create pleasure according to my own whim than be subjected to the whims of others. Invariably, I wind up entertaining others. Or educating them. There is no push/pull. It is only pull, and they do the pulling.

I find greater companionship in inert figures, animals and speechless artifacts, for I can enjoy their presence and there is no psychic drain. In fact, by their very stimulation in accordance with my tailored ideals, they provide me with not only entertainment, but food for thought.

Why do I prefer androids to many "real" humans? Androids can be created, programmed and utilized exactly according to the master's whims. They require no energy-consuming interaction in order to salve a non-existent ego. Yet even the semblance of an ego can be built into an android via actions and words — but always according to the Maker's requirements. They can be shelved when they grow tiresome, brought back out when needed, modified in appearance, and destroyed without moral conscience. They are ideal companions. They never talk back, unless you want them to, yet you can insult them to your heart's content. Insofar as work is concerned, that can be performed by either non-humanoid machines or humans of limited intelligence operating machines of greater intelligence. Androids offer splendid companion-ship when cast in the physical semblance of human beings. And for all most people really have to say, they might as well say nothing. Essen-tially, they are merely decorations in a room — humanoids to alleviate what might be construed as loneliness.

Most human interaction, being nothing more than small talk and games, is no waste of time to those so engaged. It is, in fact, necessary to their survival, for they would die of boredom otherwise. To the

Maker, the archetype, the self-sustainer, human interaction is usually a waste of the most precious thing in his vital existence: *time*. Time spent in "being liked" could better be devoted to liking *being*.

It is easy for me to expound these attitudes. I do not search for a beloved, yet am loved by one who treads the stars. In addition, I can do as well as be. I can honestly say, "I am that I am." Unless one can, he cannot be interdependent. One must be whole before one can be alone and yet not alone.

What keeps me going? What justifies my existence? That which sustains me is the knowledge that, were I to fall prey to trouble, to fail, to sicken, to die, it would please so many people that my strength is in my existence.

When I think of all those who would rejoice at my discomfort, I am energized and strengthened to the extent that I might overcome any malaise. It is not my love for mankind that sustains me, but rather mankind's resentment of me. My disdain and contempt for the mediocre masses in general and those who calumniate me in particular angers me to regeneration.

My right I have made for myself, by not what I can do, but by how important it is for others that I be resented, maligned, misunderstood and hated. You'll seldom hear me complain about my lot, for it is according to my precise design. Even if it were not, I doubt that I would gripe. I hate complainers. Nobody gives a shit about anyone else's grievances. When one caterwauls his troubles to another, it simply weakens the complainer in the listener's eyes. Far better to arouse further antagonism by disappointing your detractors by your refusal to display unease.

I refuse to sicken because it will make my enemies healthier. I refuse to break off relations with any worthwhile companion because if I did it would make others' loneliness more bearable. I refuse my sorrow to be known, for my sorrow is another's joy. I even dislike showing wrath, for to one who receives little attention, my wrath would brighten his heart.

I admire my bull terrier, Typhon, who can rage and snarl and try to kill while wagging his tail. It is patently sport — enjoyment — for him to snarl and tear at his opponent. A great lesson can be learned from him. He will not give his victim the satisfaction of thinking that, in his rage, he might be unhappy. On the contrary, he is a blight to his victim all the more because his victim can never be satisfied as a masochist is satisfied by another's drubbing. Unless you can rejoice in making your antagonist miserable, your antagonist will sap your vitality by the humorless wrath he has incurred in you. The sobriety of your anger will increase your unintended charity with each blow you strike, and you will be lesser for it. Through practice, I now enact my formula of turning rage into enjoyable sport so automatically and effortlessly, that it is seldom, if ever, possible for another to reap pleasure from my anger.

I defy ill wishes of my enemies by rejoicing in their discomfort. If I did not pain them, I should not be their enemy. If I need do nothing save exist in my present form in order to make enemies, I am indeed fortunate, for to know me is to hate me. One hates what one fears. He who is feared has power. I am lucky. I have acquired power without conscious effort, but simply by being.

I will never die because my death would enrich the unfit. I could never be that charitable.

Is it irony that the only times I have progressed is when I have hurt someone else? Or does evil really conquer goodness in the end? It appears that evil (fear) is the prime mover, while goodness is compla cency and stagnation. Goodness invokes either approbation or saccharin contempt. Evil creates action and reaction. Without that, the race would have died long ago. Not that that would have been so terrible, save it would have meant the extermination of the Devils — those persons who love life enough to want to consciously experience its pleasures, the pleasures they devise and discover on their own.

Once upon a time, when I had certain befuddled ideals, I might have found John Donne's *No Man Is An Island* justification of mediocrity inclusive of myself. "Because people need people," is now too little justification for their existence. I need persons — certain persons, not people. The word "people" has achieved an egalitarian connotation I find repugnant. —

There are some men who are islands, entire of themselves, but most are pieces of the continent — parts of the maine. If a clod — and clods they be — is washed away by the sea, the mainland is richer, albeit smaller. If a promontory were washed away, then some small alarm might be caused if one's manor built from unique efforts stood upon it. But no man's death, save he who stands by me, diminishes me. Other men's deaths make the earth a sweeter, finer place for those who have the capacity to relish each moment spent upon it. Each useless drone's death enriches me. I am involved in growth, and the incompetent dead can at best provide fertilizer. Then, though the land may be lesser in size, it will be richer in soil and lusher in visage. Therefore, never send to know for whom the bell tolls. It tolls because someone is being paid to pull on the rope.

Diabolica

I never met a person who loved everybody I didn't dislike.

🕷

What good are friends if they can't do you any good?

🕷

Man prides himself on being the only animal who can modify his nature, yet when he chooses to do so he is called a phony.

🕷

The hunter must hunt. The moment he stops he becomes the hunted.

🕷

Strive, reach, take. Then you shall not be taken.

🕷

After an inferior man has been taught a doctrine of superiority he will remain as inferior as he was before his lesson. He will merely assume himself to be superior, and attempt to employ his recently-learned tactics against his own kind, whom he will then consider his inferiors. With each inferior man enjoying what he considers his unique role, the entire bunch will be reduced to a pack of strutting, foppish, self-centered monkeys gamboling about on an island of ignorance. There they will play their games under the supervision of their keeper, who was and will always be a superior man.

🕷

Never enter a business deal with anyone who has less than yourself.

🕷

Distrust "experts" unless it is obvious that their expertise is paying off.

🕷

Be wary of advice from one who is less successful than yourself.

✻

W.C. Fields used to advise, "Never smarten up a chump." He must have known the dire consequences that can ensue when a simpleton acquires a modicum of sophistication.

The world is full of creeps. Creeps are beings who, as Thoreau said, live out their lives in quiet desperation. It is best to leave them that way, because creeps, if energized with a soupçon of self-importance, often become shit-disturbers.

Creeps can be contained and seldom cause trouble to anyone but themselves. Shit-disturbers are impossible to deal with in a civilized manner. Stay clear of shit-disturbers.

✻

Self-improvement books: those who need them won't read them or heed them.

✻

Don't help someone who has proven himself a consistent failure in the past.

✻

Definition of Good and Evil: Good is what you like. Evil is what you don't like.

✻

Too much freedom is dangerous to those who cannot cope with the responsibilities that accompany independence.

✻

The true test of anyone's worth as a living creature is how much he can utilize what he has.

✻

Those who come begging for help want to hear that I can help them. They don't really want to be helped, though. If they could stop searching for help they would die of satisfaction. I don't want to implement such dire consequences. If I even begin to help them, they will soon hate me and try to make trouble. Therefore, I tell them I will help them, sell them promises, and let them fall before their ships come in. In that way, I do truly help them. I save them for future failures.

Each misdirected act of compassion is a waste of magical energy. (Popularly expressed by the phrase, "No good deed ever goes unpunished.")

※

Anyone who retains acquaintances as friends, particularly those who are in constant disagreement with him, is either incapable of attracting anyone else, or feeding a masochistic need.

※

There are many who would take my time. I shun them.

There are some who share my time. I am entertained by them.

There are precious few who contribute to my time. I cherish them.

※

When quarreling with someone who is dear to you, transfer your mutual wrath to someone you dislike, and you will be surprised at the results.

※

Hair on a man's chest is thought to denote strength. The gorilla is the most powerful of bipeds and has hair on every place on his body except for his chest.

※

Bertrand Russell has equated logic with mathematics. I equate the brain and its potential with the thing called "soul" or "spirit."

※

Large breasts are associated with feminine women, regardless of the slenderness of their hips. The capacity of a milk container cannot be told by its outside dimensions. Femininity is more accurately displayed by generous hips. Guess you can tell I favor women with big asses.

※

The Holy Bible has been criticized by scholars because of its self-contradictions. I don't object to that, for it was designed to confound and confuse. As an historic propaganda document it is unexcelled. My objection is in its utility and re-interpretation long after its original purpose has become exhausted.

※

If self-preservation is the highest law, the "self" has its own laws which validate its existence. The first is Stimulation. The second is Identity.

※

Man is the only animal in whom the law of self-preservation is enacted after he has willingly subjected himself to the machinations of his destruction.

※

A martyr is a man who allows others to atone for their guilts by feeling sorry for him. Each constituent of the martyr enters a contest to see who can wail the loudest and the longest. The winners are those with the guiltiest conscience.

※

Control, religious or political, must exist because the populace demands to be enslaved. Only when it feels sufficiently enslaved can the dissenters produce their collective grunt. Dissension is a weak form of assertion. Assertion is a weak form of creation.

※

Egalitarianism is a condition whereby society is governed by the whim of its most inferior members, whose strength lies solely in numbers. As provender, their flesh is inferior to that of a good heifer or spring lamb. If an area of the world is a dung heap, you can be sure unprocessed egalitarians have made it so. Let such manure be spread where it will do some good.

※

Nature, in her ineffible wisdom, wastes nothing. Seemingly useless but parasitic or destructive persons should be used like clay pigeons: for target practice.

※

The most efficient street cleaner in an egalitarian society is a riot gun.

※

When people ask me, "What gives you the right to suggest standards for others?", my answer is, "If I don't, someone else, perhaps less qualified, will." History has proven that qualification is based on acceptance. The end justifies the means.

Right, like water, seeks its own level. Man's consent is not necessary to the operations of Satanic Forces. It is not required. It is not even asked.

᛭